The Desert Experience

personal reflections on finding God's
presence and promise in hard times

Tommy Barnett ✤ Jill Briscoe
Nancie Carmichael ✤ Gordon MacDonald
John C. Maxwell ✤ J. I. Packer
Charles Stanley ✤ John Trent ✤ Sheila Walsh

THOMAS NELSON PUBLISHERS
Nashville

Published in Nashville, Tennessee, by Thomas Nelson, Inc.

Scripture quotations noted NKJV are from THE NEW KING JAMES VERSION.
Copyright © 1979, 1980, 1982, Thomas Nelson, Inc., Publishers.

Scripture quotations noted NIV are from the HOLY BIBLE, NEW INTERNATIONAL
VERSION®. Copyright © 1973, 1978, 1984 by International Bible Society. Used by
permission of Zondervan Publishing House. All rights reserved.

Scripture quotations noted NASB are from the NEW AMERICAN STANDARD BIBLE ®.
Copyright © The Lockman Foundation 1960, 1962, 1963, 1968, 1971, 1972, 1973, 1975,
1977. Used by permission.

Scripture quotations noted KJV are from the King James Version.

Library of Congress Cataloging-in-Publication Data

The desert experience : personal reflections on finding God's presence and promise in
hard times / Tommy Barnett, Jill Briscoe, Nancie Carmichael [et al.].
    p. cm.
    Includes bibliographical references.
    ISBN 0-7852-6709-3 (hardcover)
    1. Encouragement—Religious aspects—Christianity. 2. Christian life. I. Barnett,
Tommy. II. Briscoe, Jill. III. Carmichael, Nancie.

BV4647.E53 D47 2001
242—dc21   00–050110

Printed in the United States of America
1 2 3 4 5 6 BVG 05 04 03 02 01

Contents

chapter *1*

DivineEraser.com

Tommy Barnett

🌿 "MAKE YOUR PLANS IN PENCIL AND GIVE GOD the eraser." Although the concept of this adage may seem simplistic, I have found—after a half century in ministry—it is valid.

One of the greatest errors an individual can commit is to assume it is impossible to make a mistake. Or that there are no desert experiences or difficulties to share and overcome. Even governments and institutions are not immune. The United States Mint made a run of gold coins imprinted with "In Gold We Trust." After more than a month on public display in the Museum of Modern Art, a famous painting was discovered to have been hung upside down. While able to recite a litany of personal shortcomings, this pastor is grateful that erasers are made for those who make mistakes or who placed too much trust in plans and dreams that may have been dashed or broken.

Experience has taught me to never undervalue God's erasers, no matter how painful the process may be. If I were to launch a Web site on my disappointments and wilderness journeys, including times of momentary depression, it would be called DivineEraser.com. Thinking back I realize now that each difficulty, each tough and challenging experience, was an opportunity for learning and growing.

In tracing life's milestones, I concur with the apostle Paul: "The things which happened to me have actually turned out for the furtherance of the gospel" (Phil. 1:12 NKJV). Yet it would be an act of omission not to be open about the hurt, humiliation, and at times, depression that occurred.

One of the most traumatic experiences for me took place about a decade ago when Phoenix First Assembly was honored, as one of the ten largest churches in the United States, to be chosen by the *Wall Street Journal* for an interview about the state of the church. The *Journal* wanted to test the current health of churches in the aftermath of the widely publicized failings of two highly visible television evangelists the previous year. By the grace of God, we were thriving, and our files and programs were opened without reservation. The preliminary information from the publisher indicated that this front-page story would be honest, positive, and fairly presented.

Instead, a degrading editorial spin placed on God's house was printed on the premier left-hand column of the front page. On the morning it appeared, a church member who watched my reaction as I read the article said it was as if all the blood drained from my body. I was livid, white-hot with anger! Why? Why such untruths? And to add insult to injury, this occurred during our Easter pageants. Each night from the platform I would welcome the vast audience of guests, many of whom were not involved in any church. How was I to face this audience? Everything within me wanted to quit. Suddenly, through the comfort of God's Word, I felt a kinship with Jeremiah. "O LORD, You induced me, and I was persuaded; / You are stronger than I, and have prevailed. / I am in derision daily; / Everyone mocks me" (Jer. 20:7 NKJV). Jeremiah went on to speak his piece in words of anger and frustration. He would scrap it all and would no longer mention the name of the Lord. Tired of rejection, he would leave his ordained post.

Jeremiah was a street preacher. Hardly anyone listened to him, and there is little recorded about any positive results. He felt equally bitter toward God's followers and sinners alike. In his readiness to surrender to defeat, I can imagine the prophet choosing a little stream with a nearby cabin to escape and leave the ministry behind.

As I walked out onto the platform the evening the article appeared in the *Journal*, I scanned the audience, thinking everyone was surely questioning the viability of Phoenix First Assembly of God. Many may have been having doubts about the work of God. Like Jeremiah, I firmly believed I had done my best, kept my life clean, and given my all. But then I felt a faint stirring of hope: maybe most of the congregation was unaware of the disparaging article. That little comfort quickly faded as I took a small, halting step of courage, gaining momentum as I walked onto the platform. Amazingly, a fire began burning within, and instantly I knew my calling would never be given up. It was a turning point and led me to research heroes of the faith and their desert times.

Since that terrifying, defining day, several hundred thousand souls have accepted Jesus Christ as their Savior at our altars or through the outreaches of the church. The prophet Jeremiah gave up, but only for a short time. I envisioned him in that cabin when the fire was rekindled in his soul and he realized there was no way for him to quit. The stream by his cabin was cathartic to a weary soul, and he later penned,

> For I know the thoughts that I think toward you, says the LORD, thoughts of peace and not of evil, to give you a future and a hope. Then you will call upon Me and go and pray to Me, and I will listen to you. And you will seek Me and find Me, when you search for Me with all your heart. (Jer. 29:11–13 NKJV)

There Is Life After Giving Up

With the Bible as a model, greater levels of faith can be attained when considering another Old Testament prophet, Elijah. He was an incredible fellow, an intense individual who was capable of extreme exhilaration. A leader of men, whose physical fitness was never in doubt, he was not dependent on his friends. Remember how he outran a chariot? Historians relate that he possessed a solitary grandeur while he walked in mystery. He had a heavenly name accompanied by a very earthly nature.

Alexander Whyte offered this description: "Elijah was a great man. There was a great mass of manhood in Elijah. He was a Mount Sinai of man, with a heart like a thunderstorm. A passion of scorn and contempt; a passion of anger and revenge; a passion of sadness, dejection and despair; a passion of preaching; a passion of prayer." Is this not a description of the life and times of a preacher? Elijah had seen the hand of God in defeat and in triumph. His faith moved mountains, but conversely, at times he was in the depths of despair.

Scripture informs us that Elijah felt a particular responsibility to prove to the Israelite people that Jehovah was God and that Baal was an ineffective fake. He carried out that responsibility with all the tension of a suspense drama. However, after his great success, he was confronted by Jezebel, a powerful woman who hated him for embarrassing Baal's followers and killing the false religious leaders. Elijah suffered total depression in the wake of Jezebel's threats. Even though he had wit-

nessed God's defeat of more than 450 prophets of Baal,
Jezebel's anger reduced him to putty and he was unwilling to stand up to her.

First Kings 18 and 19 narrate this interesting and
enlightening saga of Elijah's blues under the juniper tree
and his encounter with God. Amid those debilitating
"juniper blues," Elijah railed against God in a drastic dialogue. How distraught he must have been to question
God's power!

Elijah asked for death, but was granted renewal of his
life. God provided physical sustenance. Yet food and rest
were not enough; Elijah needed spiritual nourishment
as well. He spilled out his heart's innermost thoughts.
The Lord let him talk, then asked some rather humiliat-
ing questions: What are you doing here? Why are you
sitting under that juniper tree? Why are you so sub-
merged in the burdens of the day?

Elijah's answer resonates with the classic response of
many depressed and discouraged believers: "I am all
alone!" (Much the same way I felt prior to walking onto
that platform after the *Wall Street Journal*'s diatribe!)

Had God been unfaithful to Elijah? A resounding no!
"All the promises of God in Him are Yes, and in Him

Amen" (2 Cor. 1:20 NKJV). Had he not seen the power of God's working at Cherith? His provision for the widow at Zarephath? The glorious victory on Carmel? Would God forsake Elijah now? Never. Nor did He forsake this humble servant on the Easter pageant platform years ago.

Both Elijah and I were reminded that we were not alone. For Elijah, God told him there were seven thousand others who also were faithful. Though centuries apart, both of us recognized that *there is life after giving up.*

Depression and wilderness experiences mean different things to different people. When pessimism and sadness prevail for no apparent reason, there must come a time of concentration on "soaring spirits." Physicians agree that "the best known fact of depression is recoverability." The Christian is offered recoverability with divine dimension. Even when asking for death, there is life with a capital "L." Our Lord's heart is touched with our grief, and He is ever listening. Psalm 84:6 (NKJV) beautifully relates, "As they pass through the Valley of Baca [weeping and sadness], / They make it a spring"— a well of living, life-rejuvenating waters.

Please do not misunderstand. Christianity is not an escape from reality . . . it is *true* reality. Christ does not promise to ban potential "juniper blues" as His servant Elijah suffered, but to provide an antidote for them. There is life after giving up—by being heaven-born and heaven-bound, and doing God's works—works that may go unnoticed here, but not in the hereafter.

There Is Life After Giving Up
Even on Your Dreams

God is a God of everything but failure. That is why He graciously responds, "Though he fall, he shall not be utterly cast down; / For the LORD upholds him with His hand" (Ps. 37:24 NKJV).

Part of my dream in coming to Phoenix years ago was to build a modest prayer chapel halfway up the mountain where our church is situated. It was designed to be the focal point of a wonderful garden, surrounded by cacti in all its natural splendor. Designed for God's glory, the chapel was to be a symbol to the community that people would be praying around the clock on the mountainside. The Shadow Mountains afforded the opportunity of literally living in the "shadow" of the Almighty. I clearly envisioned that this would become a symbol to people driving by, noticing the cross in place and causing them to think of God.

For years I shared the dream with the congregation and they became excited and supported the project. The notes accompanying the gifts were heartening, from the poorest of the poor to the more affluent.

However, something went wrong. On receiving our building plans, the city responded that they were condemning eleven acres on the side of the mountain to be designated as a mountain preserve—precisely the eleven acres belonging to the church. I talked to the Lord, attorneys, and godly advisers. It felt as if my heart had fled and fallen on hard rocks in a deep valley of depression.

During an opportunity to share the vision with the city council, I emphasized that our dream would not destroy the mountain, but would be a valuable asset for the city as well as the telephone crisis lines. People would be fed, clothed, and their hurts would be helped. Encouraged, I left the meeting believing some had been responsive. The following day the newspapers trumpeted on the editorial page that a seventy-foot tower defacing the mountain was being proposed. Yet there was never any kind of towering spire in our building plans.

Calls were placed to the newspapers and environmentalists to try to set the record straight. Although the facts as published were patently false, the newspapers would not retract the story. Things took a turn for the worse when a cartoon of a crown forming a distorted prayer chapel appeared. Topping the crown was a spire embellished with a dollar sign. The caption, "First Assembly of Tommy Barnett," was the greatest heartbreak of all.

The misleading campaign continued, and had it not been for God's strength and the support of our people, I may have been reluctant to accept the comforting truth of God's Word: "When my heart is overwhelmed; / Lead me to the rock that is higher than I" (Ps. 61:2 NKJV). The Rock that is higher than my dreams, hopes, or expectations. Surely our Gibraltar—the Rock of Ages— was not caught off-guard at the unfairness of an untruthful press and the results of the "council of the ungodly."

There is no doubt that we got a bad rap. However, we serve a sovereign God, and His purposes continued to build our church. Why? Because Jesus never fails! He can do everything but fail! He is on the corner before we are, and His ultimate purpose will never be thwarted. There are times when God says no, as He did to His own Son when Jesus prayed, "Let this cup pass from Me; nevertheless, not as I will, but as You will" (Matt. 26:39 NKJV). That was the most important prayer in history. There are many "whys" when referring to unanswered prayers, but they begin to dissolve when we remember that all of our whys should end at Calvary.

I thank God that His ways are not my ways. There have been many prayers and no answers, but He is the final authority and has the right to use His "eraser." What an incredible asset to know He allows us instant access to Him. I have the living Lord's ear; I have His attention and it costs me nothing. He paid that fee when He died on the cross. There was no reason to feel strange when the Lord answered no to the chapel. He answered no to Jesus also.

God's ways are not like human ways,
He wears such strange disguises.
He tries us by His long delays and then our faith surprises.
When we, in unbelief, deplore and wonder at His staying,
He stands already at the door to interrupt our praying.

Currently, the Dream Center is transforming the ninth floor into a "prayer terrace." It will potentially be visible to twenty million people, to the glory of God, far surpassing the outreach of the mountainside chapel in Phoenix. Delay was not denial.

Looking at the ashes of the great Chicago fire, D. L. Moody saw a Bible institute, a place to train missionaries and pastors; to publish books and do good. Remembering his struggles provided perspective for my disappointments. Moody's vision stands today as a great asset to the work of the Lord and science. My dream did not die in the arms of those people who believed lies. It is still alive and has since been transferred into a vision of unbelievable growth. Through the experience, God has taken the plans for a small chapel and replaced them with unexpected programs.

With all glory and honor to the Lord, just a few years ago the Los Angeles International Church was born and there are Dream Centers growing around the world, ministering to inner cities and changing lives that were once without hope.

God has provided a pastor's college at Phoenix First to challenge many. For more than a decade, our pastor's schools have grown beyond description. Since that difficult period we have moved into gigantic building programs that will care for upward of twenty thousand by the end of the year 2000. Yes, there is life after Satan's attempt to dishearten and discourage one to give up.

There Is Life After Messing Up

My son, Matthew, who is pastoring the Los Angeles church, and I often stand in awe of the joy of witnessing this truth.

Former gang members, prostitutes, homeless people, and runaways are experiencing the One who spoke, "I am come that you might have life and have it more abundantly." Teaching the truth of God's inspired Word with examples from the past and the present is the assurance of new life after messing up.

At the Dream Center campus I was sitting in the car, bone-tired from weeks on the road to raise funds for the Los Angeles ministry, when I recognized a radiant young woman. She had been a prostitute working the Los Angeles streets, but had been delivered from the bondage of drugs and her lifestyle. She had completed the discipleship program and was surrounded by Christian friends.

Then Billy Soto walked out through the front doors; the tattoos covering his arms mirror the story of his past—thirty years of addictions and living on the streets. Today, Billy is free, born again. He ministers to AIDS victims and the homeless living under the bridges of Los Angeles. His wife and children followed, all having been restored and reunited as a family. They live at the Dream Center and minister to hurting people.

A former "crack mama," severely abused by her husband, had met Jesus through the Los Angeles project. We put feet to our prayers for her husband, and his life was also dramatically changed. Now both are serving the Lord.

Yes, there is life after sin and abuse. My weariness was reinvigorated. The desert wilderness of raising money, meeting needs, healing hurts, facing lies and bureaucracy becomes insignificant when faced with the glory set before us. The only thing we can take to heaven with us is people, changed by the blood of the Lamb.

One can identify with Martin Luther, who, obviously fighting the good fight, became depressed and, like many, wanted to give up. He was so frustrated with the devil that he threw his inkwell at the wall where he felt Satan's image. It left an indelible mark, which Luther never permitted to be removed or covered because it reminded him not to give up and to never question again what he had been called to do. When detractors came to take him to the Diet of Worms, he doubled his fist and made his statement. How else would he have experienced that "the just shall live by his faith" (Hab. 2:4 NKJV)? Because he would not be daunted, the Great Reformation followed.

In reviewing biblical individuals, I recalled David's "messing up." He sent a man to fight a war in full knowledge that death in battle would be the result. Then he married the slain man's wife, Bathsheba. Tragedy followed tragedy in his family as a result. He experienced failure with his children. One raped his own half sister and was in turn killed by another brother in revenge. Another attempted to overthrow his father in a political insurrection. In spite of messing up big-time, David got right with God. It is always heartening to read that, prior to these occurrences, David penned his words and referred to "our God." After experiencing the personal presence and full assurance of God's forgiveness, then he changed it to "my God." David was a man after God's own heart.

There is a simple, childlike definition of faith, the kind of faith that impelled Martin Luther to move forward: "Faith is believing God and asking no questions." This is exactly what it is, taking almighty God at His word. Hebrews 11:1 clarifies this truth: "Now faith is the substance of things hoped for, the evidence of things not seen" (NKJV). God knows beyond man's understanding. Faith gives substance to that truth. The Puritans wrote that "it makes unseen things even more real than things that the eye beholds. It relies with unquestioning certainty there is this complete reliance upon the promises of God." In other words, whether wanting to give up or having messed up, "[God] is faithful and just to forgive us our sins and to cleanse us from all unrighteousness" (1 John 1:9 NKJV). A fresh start and new beginning are available.

Mary Magdalene in the New Testament plied the world's oldest profession, selling herself. After coming to Jesus, she later washed His feet with her hair, and led many to faith.

Samson experienced new life after messing up. A muscular Don Juan, he was one of the Judges. It is said of him that, after his sin—his involvement with the wrong woman—he lost his legendary strength, and his sight and soul were marred; then "the Spirit of the Lord came upon him and he destroyed more of the enemy in death than in life."

Countless others can testify that they have experienced God and found Him sufficient. It is a message that is needed as we move into the twenty-first century. Depression and suicide are rampant. America is affluent for many, yet discouragement and debilitating wilderness experiences are an increasingly equal-opportunity plague. Even within the church we have become a lonely nation in spite of cell phones, mass transportation, and unlimited communication, and we rarely know those who sit in the pew beside us. People are ever more stressed out even though the Dow is up and the Balkan crisis is winding down. There is an explosion of crisis counselors, mood-altering drugs, and Columbine-style tragedies. Is there hope? Is there recoverability from depression, or desert or wilderness experiences?

Spurgeon wrote, "God's inexhaustible fullness is treasured up where all the needy may reach it, in Christ." Where did he find such strength after being kicked out of the Baptist denominations? In God's Word and promises! Consider John Bunyan. He had every reason to be depressed and discouraged. He preached on the streets and was thrown into prison, but a prisoner he was not! On the back of milk bottle stops he wrote *Pilgrim's Progress,* the number two best-seller, next to the Bible.

Ironically, difficulties can bring greater relief in the power and purposes of God. People can rise above setbacks and sin, and move forward through the message of the Cross. It has been my personal experience that "we are more than conquerors through Him who loved us" (Rom. 8:37 NKJV). That is what resurrection is all about—rising above ourselves and circumstances, and by faith, being welcomed into the kingdom of God, reaching for that "inexhaustible fullness."

"Whosoever will." This message is written to all those perceived worthless, with no self-esteem, knocked down or bankrupt in every way. We must all be reminded that Jesus never gave up on us. He not only went to the

cross, He died for us and then overcame death. His tomb
is empty! There is no place to lay commemorative flowers on His grave because death could not hold Him. Our
best bouquets are those symbolizing that there is life
after giving up, life after messing up, life after depression
and pain and wilderness journeys. A worthy offering to
present to Him is one with stems rooted in the
Resurrection. He overcame, and we can too.

Many outreaches, even churches today, tend to recy-
cle everything except people. We criticize and trod on
those who need to be restored to a new life. It is easy to
ridicule and repeat the failures of others. Recycling, in
the name of Jesus Christ, is what our church is all about.
However, there are times when firm decisions create difficulty for some.

The newspaper carried a story of a woman who was
despondent about her and her children's future. A living
portrait of depression, she found herself on the edge of
oblivion, with no hope on the horizon. In a moment of
terror, she doused the children and herself with gaso-
line and struck the match. She and one youngster survived the conflagration. The courts made a decision to
let her live; though her body was fragile and wasted.

One of our hospital visitation pastors went to see her, much to the shock of the staff where she was housed. It was the first visit by an outsider to her sequestered living quarters. While not prepared for the ravages of such a badly burned body, the visiting individual nevertheless came bearing a gift of hope: "Though our outward man is perishing, yet the inward man is being renewed day by day" (2 Cor. 4:16 NKJV). He shared that Jesus loved her. On hearing there was life after giving up and messing up, she yielded her heart to the Lord.

While she did not believe she would ever be able to attend church, we made it possible. With no hands or ears, her feet burned off, and only a couple of holes for breathing, she came and joined us in worshiping the risen Christ, her newly discovered Savior. She has come to understand that God is a thousand times more merciful than He is judgmental. The act she committed was horrific, but not beyond the realm of mercy and forgiveness of a loving God. Our buildings are hospitals for the sick and depressed, the lonely and the active. Why? Many have experienced genuine life after giving up, new life after messing up, and life after being knocked down, but not quite out.

Most disappointments we face become God's appointments. Many of the heartaches and setbacks I have experienced have turned out to be great sermon illustrations for the future. Upon finding myself floundering, beaten up, and at times, bedraggled, I rush toward the high road . . . the road to praise. You see, "He is your praise, and He is your God, who has done for you these great and awesome things which your eyes have seen" (Deut. 10:21 NKJV). My eyes have seen. "Blessed are those who have not seen and yet have believed" (John 20:29 NKJV).

What a legacy is ours in Christ! To write our plans in pencil and give God the eraser is a simple sacrifice of implicit trust and obedience. Each believer is called to be a prover of God, making the Bible as relevant as today's news . . . and much more. We must make Jesus so real that He will break out of the Book into live action, by demonstrating who He is and His life-changing mission. This world may be skeptical, but I know beyond a doubt that my faith was forged into stronger substance because of wilderness experiences. Through it all, I act on the unalterable belief that "He who is in [me] is greater than he who is in the world" (1 John 4:4 NKJV).

chapter 2

You Should Have Come Sooner

Jill Briscoe

❦ I WAS BUSY. REALLY BUSY. THAT WAS A GOOD FEELING. In fact it was almost a necessity, seeing that my husband was on the road most of the time. We were in Britain in full-time Christian work—very full-time. One of the sayings of our mission was, "Soldiers of Jesus Christ are on duty twenty-four hours a day, seven days a week." Maybe this sounds a bit extreme, but my husband, Stuart, and I were in a Christian culture whose favorite hymn was, "Let us burn out for Thee, Lord Jesus."

It wasn't until I came to America and saw seminars being offered on burnout that I recognized what was happening to me over and over again. Not that I had burned out physically, but rather spiritually. This was no one's fault but my own. The mission leaders certainly had spoken strongly about keeping fresh in ministry, and had given us all the encouragement in the world to do so.

Every week during the short-term Bible schools that were run at the center, a guest speaker would teach the Bible, and the staff were always welcome to take advantage of this. I hardly ever did. My excuses ranged from not being able to find a baby-sitter for our three children to busying myself with my own ministry to the women and youth in the area.

I had three different translations of the Bible on my shelves and one on my bedside, and a library of Christian books. Few had been read. As a result, I felt like a flat camel! The nourishment that should have been stored in my hump was gone! I would be on duty during church service so I would seldom even get in to the chapel to participate in the corporate worship.

So I was busy. And it was all really good stuff. Spiritual stuff. But it was all output and little or no intake. The inevitable result was a desert experience. This was serious because I was under considerable stress with a spouse who was home very little of the time and three small children under school age.

The drier I got, the more irritating my children seemed

to become. "My kids are driving me crazy," I complained to a friend. "Jill," she said gently, "your children don't create your attitude, they reveal it!" Ouch, that was too close to home. I knew she was right. After all, a cup filled with sweet water when jogged cannot spill one bitter drop!

When you are in a desert and you are thirsty you can begin to see mirages. I began to see things that weren't real. Satan aided in this. "Everything is fine," he assured me. "Just look at all the things you've got going. Why, you have a meeting every night of the week, and people are coming to the house day and night to get help. Don't stop doing what you are doing," he intoned in my ear. "In fact you could squeeze a couple of more things in on your only day off." I listened and complied, not recognizing his voice. After all, surely there was spiritual merit in burning out for Jesus.

"Actually there is greater merit in burning *on* for Jesus," whispered the Spirit of God in my ear, but I thought the still, small whisper was the wind as I continually rushed up the road between our home and the youth center.

Busyness doesn't have to be wrong. It is busyness

God has not authorized that is wrong. Jesus said, "I must work the works of Him that sent Me while it is day; the night comes when no one can work." He said, "My Father is working to this day, and I, too, must work." At the end of His life He was able to say, "I have finished the work You gave Me to do." Note that He finished the work His Father had given *Him* to do. Not the work His Father had given everyone else to do!

Jesus also said, "Man shall not live by bread alone, but by every word that proceeds from the mouth of God" (Matt. 4:4 NKJV). It is from the Word of God that we find out what work God wants us to do! We can't figure it out for ourselves. If we are not in the Word of God then the "tyranny of the urgent" will rule. Jesus spent whole nights in prayer and said, "Men ought always to pray, and not to faint" (Luke 18:1 KJV). There is one thing for sure: if we don't pray we will faint!

Once when Jesus' disciples were strung out with the demands of the ministry, Jesus said to them, "Come apart and rest awhile" (see Mark 6:31). He knew that if they didn't come apart they would surely come apart! But how to do it when the demands are so obvious and people are so needy? How do we draw aside and learn the art of leaving things undone in order that the greater thing be done? I didn't know, and I didn't do it until trouble forced me to confront the issue.

Trouble came to me in a series of difficult things that happened. First my dad got cancer. This was incredibly painful; watching a beloved parent slowly disintegrate before your eyes takes a toll. Then our daughter broke her arm the day after Stuart left for a long road trip. I hurt my back quite seriously, and on top of all this we had a series of threats from some dangerous kids we had been working with. One of these doubtful characters had just gotten out of jail and insisted on knocking on our windows at night to scare us. Suddenly the long absences of my husband on ministry business became overwhelming, and the accumulated pressure became unbearable. I found out to my chagrin that I was not the good little missionary wife I had thought I was!

Resentment that had been festering in my heart began to surface, and I realized a whole lot of issues lay unresolved. Of course I hadn't taken time out with the Lord to resolve them, so they had steadily built up and now began to spill over into daily life. They began to be vented on my friends and family who seemed powerless to help me.

This desert of spiritual despondency was dry and hot and made me oh-so-thirsty for a cup of cold water from the spring of living waters. One day as I washed the dishes and dressed my kids, God brought the story of Hagar to mind. My hands busy, my mind rehearsed the narrative. The woman was in a tough spot, having run away from Sarai, who was mistreating her. A desert without water is serious business, and Hagar ran on till she found a well. It was providential because, pregnant and alone, Hagar was prey to dehydration and marauders. It was in a desert of her own making that she found the life-giving water. It was at the well that she heard the voice of the Lord, "Hagar, Sarai's maid, where have you come from, and where are you going?" (Gen. 16:8 NKJV). It was not that God was ignorant of her movements; He wanted to engage her in dialogue. He wanted her to talk to Him. He wanted to tell her He loved her as much as He loved Abraham and Sarai, her mistress, and He wanted to save her life and the life of the child she had jeopardized through the action she had taken.

Hagar drank at the well. Water—life-giving, sustaining water—saved her life, and she went home to less-than-favorable circumstances, refreshed by the incredible experience of meeting the "living God" who knew her name, her dilemma, and had her in the palm of His hand.

As I tied a small, wiggling child's shoelaces I knew what God was telling me. I needed a "Hagar" experience. I couldn't remember how long it had been since I had heard His voice, *really* heard His voice. Even as I readied my children for school, I was suddenly made aware of a terrible inner want—a thirst for God and for a fresh touch of His life.

I would not perhaps have come to this place if it hadn't been for the problems that God had allowed to come into my life. So I allowed the hurts to drive me to God, and He dealt with me as gently as He dealt with Hagar, and so my healing began.

The first thing I did was reinstate my time with God that had fallen into disrepair. I began to visit the Well on a daily basis. It was a matter of reforming a habit.

Discipline came hard to me, especially after such a long dry spell, but I set myself down after lunch every day when I had a small window of respite from the children, and it wasn't long before I heard the still, small voice whisper, "You should have come sooner." He was right, I should have. But then it often takes pain or pressure to drive us to God. It was desperation in my case. I couldn't cope anymore.

I had hardly begun my times with the Lord again when I read in my respite time, "How shall we escape if we neglect so great a salvation?" (Heb. 2:3 NKJV). This passage convicted me. I was neglecting the great salvation gift I had been given. I cried as the Word went deep and God began to deal with me. It was the start of a brand-new day!

The Word leaped to life as God and I began to talk about many things together. I couldn't wait until lunchtime, so I left a Bible open on the kitchen counter so I could snatch a blade or two of grass from the green pastures as I whipped past on some domestic duty during the day before our precious rendezvous. A notebook lay open beside the Scriptures so I could capture a thought or idea to be expanded upon at lunchtime.

It wasn't till a few weeks into this routine that I realized I had begun to fast in order to have as much time as possible. I had a simple choice: spend the precious, limited moments making myself a sandwich and a cup of tea and minimize my time with the Lord, or forget the sandwich and maximize the few moments that He and I had. So I was introduced to the concept of fasting in order to keep nourished spiritually. It has stood me in good stead ever since.

Next I found corners around the house where I could leave a Bible open with a notebook and pencil at hand, and I wrote God little notes of appreciation, captured a Scripture that came to mind, or jotted down a child's need on the run. The kids sometimes added their little comments on the pages. They were precious. It is amazing how much truth can be gleaned from the corners of a field before the day is through.

My desert began to blossom like a rose. And I was not the only one who noticed the difference. "You are a nicer mommy," Judy commented one day. This from a four-year-old who was watching me without knowing she was! I was discovering that being a nice mommy under pressure takes as much power as preaching to thousands of people, and I have done both. When you are shut up with small children and you are not very happy with your lot in life, you need to drink often at the Well in order to stay fresh and sweet in the heat of the day.

I learned the secret of contentment in those days. As Paul found, the content of contentment is Christ! (Phil. 4:12–13 NKJV). I knew in my head that no man could ever love me enough, no child could ever need me enough, no friend could ever befriend me enough— only Jesus could! But now I began to know that fact as a reality in my heart.

I remember sitting by our coal fire in our small house in the sprawling country grounds near our youth center. There were a whole lot of things seriously wrong with my world. I should have been really lonely, as Stuart had just gone on a three-month worldwide ministry tour. Yet there was an almost luminous Presence that moved in with me when Stuart moved out that never seemed to be there when my husband was at home! I had enormous pressures for a young mother of three preschoolers, and I tried to be appropriately concerned about the state of affairs I found myself in. But for the life of me I couldn't do it. Jesus was far too near and far too dear to me in those wonderful days of spiritual reality to let me be sorry for myself or in fact be worried about anything. My soul was laughing and my spirit tap-dancing! Only God can dig a well that deep in your soul!

It was on that particular night that our young friend from the youth group who had just gotten out of prison chose to do a bit of "Jill terrorizing," and I heard knocking on the windows. I knew it was him as he had threatened to pay us a visit. I was knitting by the fire in the small lodge that was our home, and our three little ones were tucked up snugly in bed. Stuart was in Australia, literally on the other side of the world, and the country police station was six miles away and our policeman had only a bike! Initially my heart raced and my knitting needles clacked rapidly against each other. Then I prayed, "Help, Lord." "Surely," He replied.

Trying to ignore the knocking, I opened my Bible to the story of David and Goliath and read it. I didn't have David's nerve, and I didn't have a sling, but I did have a fire poker and the same Captain of the Lord of Hosts on my side.

I found myself incredibly calm and quite sure what I

must do. I waited at the back door and slid back the lock. When he got around to my side of the house I opened the door in his face, screamed at him at the top of my lungs, and went for him with the poker. I took a swipe at thin air and then the poker connected with his backside as he ran into the bushes. I went back inside the house, locked the door, and called the police. The policeman laughed when I told him what had happened. "He won't bother you again," he said, and he didn't. Shortly after he was caught breaking and entering a house, and this time went down for a long time.

That night I had one of the sweetest times of my life with the Lord. His presence was so evident in my little room that I kept looking around to see Him there. To be as happy with the problems of life as without them is to find the oasis of the Spirit in the deserts of your life.

But even though I thought I had learned my lesson, it was not long after this that I allowed my spiritual disciplines to slip again. I stopped visiting the Well and allowed the barrenness of busyness to take over one more time.

My problems were moderately under control, and so

I stepped up the ante at the mission center. I added all sorts of activities to an already overloaded schedule and set to work. I enjoyed everything I was doing and shut my ears to the still, small voice telling me I had become more enamored with the work of the Lord than with the Lord of the work! Like Martha in Luke 10:40, I had allowed myself to become "distracted with much serving" (NKJV).

Being Martha instead of Mary is a battle I still fight. Being a task-oriented person, it is so hard to stop in the middle of the muddle in order to listen to Him. But if you don't stop in the middle of the muddle, you will find you soon have a muddle in your middle! Being Martha-like ties your stomach in knots.

Once again I experienced what it is like to see the work of God blossoming all around me and yet to know a growing weariness inside as time with Him diminished. But I plowed on regardless, ignoring the warning signs of spiritual fatigue that surfaced. One day, driven by guilt to have a rare quiet time, I read the story of Elijah under his proverbial broom tree and recognized myself.

"I have had enough, Lord," Elijah complained, and I

echoed his sentiments (see 1 Kings 19:4). I, too, "had had it, Lord," with the mission, with the long absences of my husband, with the struggle of raising three small children with a daddy space in their lives. I had a growing consciousness that I had failed everyone, including God Himself. I couldn't do it anymore. Flat on my face in my desert of despair I gave up, whereupon I'm sure I heard a cheerful "At last!" from the general vicinity of heaven!

In my desert of despondency I learned the life message that the basis of all spiritual strength is helplessness and dependence, and so God was not surprised at my desperate "I've had it, Lord" cry. On the contrary, He had been waiting around the corner of my self-effort to see me come to "wit's end corner" and throw myself on Him. I discovered right then that He would bake me bread and quench my thirst in whatever desert of my own making I landed in, just as He did for Elijah (2 Kings 19:6–8).

Once more I realized that I had been distracted by doing things for God. Good things, God's things, but not the things He had directed me to do! Being busy had become synonymous with being spiritual. Every time there was church I was there. Each time a volunteer was appealed for I responded. I joined a service organization in town so I could do evangelism and began to roam the streets at night with groups of Bible school students on outreach when my children were in bed. I added hours to my volunteer time at the children's preschool and then went a step further and opened my own Christian day school, ending up with two hundred students! And all this without drinking at the Well. "No wonder you ended up under the proverbial broom tree, Jill," I can hear you saying.

Yet I handled all the outside activity moderately well. It was the inactivity in my spirit that took me down. When God is busy in your life, the service flows out naturally. You are renewed day by day. It is simple then to know when to say no and when to say yes. When the Bible is open again and you are open to the Bible, then the dynamism of the Spirit drives the engine and not self-power. You are not stoking the engine, He is. The difference is dramatic.

I didn't stay under the broom tree long. It was too hot and hopeless there. Refreshed by the Lord's loving concern, "The journey is too great for you" (1 Kings 19:7

NKJV), I journeyed on in His power, better for one more reminder that I could not live the Christian life all by myself. It was not a matter of living it for Him, but rather by Him and through Him.

How often do we need to learn the same lesson? Spiritual dryness dogged me through those mission days. Over and over, or so it seemed, I ended up in the same dry place I had already experienced. I came to realize God was readying me for a greater field of service and this one abiding lesson *must* be learned if I was to be of any use to Him in the future.

I had no idea that the future would involve emigrating to America and a brand-new life and ministry that would eventually take me around the world. But I became aware that something was going on in my apprenticeship that was the most important thing I needed to learn. Yes, it was important to learn ministry skills, and of course I needed to hone and sharpen my gifts and talents, but the greatest necessity was to learn God!

Deserts would come and go. The desert of death, the desert of opposition and criticism, the desert of fear and pain, the desert of obsessive worry about my kids. But no desert was as important as this one was. The desert of "doing" would be my undoing before any of the other places of testing. "Doing without being" could finish me off all together.

So a great prayer adventure began all those years ago in England, and thirty years later is still going on. For prayer, I knew, would be the means of attaining a freshness in the Spirit that would stop my drinking from all the leaking wells that the church, the world, or the devil would continue to offer me. The cry of my heart was this: "I want to know Christ and the power of his resurrection and the fellowship of sharing in his sufferings, becoming like him in his death" (Phil. 3:10–11 NIV).

Knowing Christ doesn't mean "coming" to know Him, it means "getting" to know Him. Getting to know Him better. Getting to know Him until you are down on your knees with your face to the rising Son and never wanting to get up again. Getting to know Him until He is the most precious Person that you know.

It means getting to know His power in your life. Fresh, potent power that signals you out from the generic Christian pack. Power to minister grace to a hurt and dying world. Grace to have words of comfort not a curse, words of healing not of hurt, words of fire and life.

It means understanding a little of the sufferings of Christ when you are rejected for His sake. When you are not appreciated, thanked, or applauded. When others impinge your motives when you know you have done your level best to do the right thing. When life is not fair, glance heavenward and see Him smile and it will be enough. He understands.

And knowing Christ means being Christ-centric and not egocentric. Dying to yourself and living to Him, for Him, and through Him.

I have an insatiable thirst to so know Christ. And, strangely enough, while I am thirsty to so know Him I find I am not thirsty at all, for I am drinking at the Well and I care not where I am, how I am, or who I am. Only Jesus matters!

It all comes down to today. After all, we only have today. We don't have all the yesterdays when we learned our desert lessons or all the tomorrows when we may well find ourselves under some broom tree or other; we only have the gift of today. Day by day we make a daily choice to meet with Him about the day He has gifted us with! Will we do it?

I went to the Well today. It was wonderful. We talked

secrets He and I, the Lover of my soul. And He thanked me for coming. "You should have come sooner," He said. He was right, of course; I should have. My loss! What a Savior, what a Friend, what an incredible Jesus!

chapter 3

The Gift of the Desert

Nancie Carmichael

> Why do You stand afar off, O LORD?
> Why do You hide in times of trouble?
>
> —Psalm 10:1 NKJV

❦ IN MY LATE THIRTIES, I BECAME CONSUMED WITH the thought that I no longer wanted to live. The thought would reverberate inside my head, and I would say it at times, even aloud to my husband: "You would be better off without me. I wish I could die." And he would recoil. "Don't *say* that! You don't mean it." I *do,* I would insist inwardly. The despair inside was real. I had gone from being a healthy and confident woman to being physically and emotionally ill.

Outwardly, I seemed to function: the wife of a busy publisher, mother of five handsome and vital children, leader in church activities. One day I gave a luncheon in my home and a friend told me later that as she drove away with another friend who was also there, the woman remarked, "Nancie has the perfect life. I wish I could be like her." She had no idea what I was experiencing.

In some ways writing about this has been painful because I had to relive some of the emotions of that time. Why did I go through this difficult experience? Probably many reasons, some of which I may never know. Certainly the desert experience is part of being human, and we all experience it in some form, sooner or later. As Ecclesiastes 9:11 says, "The race is not to the swift, / Nor the battle to the strong, / Nor bread to the wise, / Nor riches to men of understanding, / Nor favor to men of skill; / But time and chance happen to them all" (NKJV).

🌿 🌿 🌿

I married early at the age of eighteen after one year of college, and although I was young, I thought I was ready for life as long as I had my wonderful Bill by my side. I had always loved learning and had been an honor student in high school, but after we married, Bill enrolled in graduate school so I put my schooling on hold, thinking I would come back to it someday. I got a job to help him get through.

Soon, life just began happening to me. We had our first child, and then Bill took a position in a church. After eight years we had four very active sons, and we were all the while immersed in pastoring and missions work. Bill started a magazine for a missions organization and realized he had found a niche that challenged his entrepreneurial and organizational skills. With my lifelong love for writing, I was right beside him, doing book reviews and articles, meanwhile juggling the home front. To say life was busy would be an understatement.

We decided to give publishing our full efforts, so we resigned from our church involvements and moved to a beautiful little mountain community to begin our own publishing venture. Our plan was to "simplify life": we cut our own wood to heat our house; I would make homemade bread and soup on our woodstove and give our growing sons quality time. And at first, it was an idyllic existence. We felt sheltered and protected, and the small community was a wonderful place for our growing family.

The only problem with escaping to the woods is that we brought ourselves with us, and before too many years, we had three magazines and a staff of more than forty people.

🌿 🌿 🌿

My journey into the desert took some time, and although I wasn't aware that it was closing around me, it hit me full force by 1985. I believe the seeds for it had started six years earlier with the death of my father. My mother also had cancer and was undergoing chemotherapy when my father died. I thought somehow I needed to be strong for her, and so I swallowed my tears for my father, even doing the music for both of my father's funerals—one in Oregon and the final one at our Montana home. *Daddy's not dead,* I wrote rather grandly in my journal. *He's alive now more than the rest of us. He's just not here.* Which is true with eyes of faith, but it shows my state of mind—I was denying the real pain of a very real loss.

I worried over my mother's fragile condition. Mother was extremely important in my life—more than a close friend. How could I live without her too? I became consumed with the thought that if I had a daughter, she would fill up the hole my mother would leave. Since we were unable to have any more biological children, I latched on to the idea of adopting a daughter. I rationalized, "There are many motherless daughters; and I need a daughter—so it's logical—we'll adopt."

As I look back now, I realize that I was protecting myself from the pain of loss by trying to build the perfect life.

❧ ❧ ❧

Our three-and-a-half-year-old daughter—Kim Yung Ja—arrived from Korea on a Northwest Orient plane from Seoul at Seattle's airport in February 1984, and Bill and I and our sons were there to meet her. I thought, *At last—the daughter of my heart! Sure, we may have challenges, but love will conquer all.* We named her Amy Carmichael after the renowned missionary to India, and we proceeded to get acquainted. As months went by, it became evident that she had some very complex learning disabilities from encephalitis that she'd had while in the orphanage, and the lack of early nurturing had left some very deep holes that were difficult to fill.

During this time I began to suffer physically. My immune system took a jolt when I developed toxic shock syndrome. I recovered initially, but shortly after, it seemed I couldn't get well. A year, then two years, passed during which I had frequent low-grade fevers, chronic pain in my joints, and mind-numbing fatigue. But the worst was the paralyzing depression.

I wrote in my journal,

> Had tests at the lab this morning and will go back later to see if there's some physical reason for the way I feel. What is wrong with me? Every day I search for a Scripture that will help me get through the day: "God will supply my every need" or, "I can do all things through Christ." But there are some days I cannot even grasp hold of a Scripture or thought and I feel as though I'm at the bottom of a well, screaming "Help!" to the top.

At first there seemed to be no diagnosis, and I tried different medications. The side effects of the drugs at times were troublesome, and I would try something else. Finally, after more tests and seeing different specialists, my doctor told me he thought I had systemic lupus erythematosus, an autoimmune disease. Having a diagnosis—even though I was dismayed at having lupus—was a relief. At least I had a label, although the idea of a "chronic" condition bothered me. I wanted to get over it; I had things to do.

"I'd Quit, If I Knew How . . ."

During this time Bill was incredibly busy trying to build a magazine company. He included me in the venture and I enjoyed the challenge of it, but I felt I was losing him too. My illness was hard on Bill, as he is the kind of man who can fix anything—but he couldn't fix me, and he was worried and frustrated. I'm sure it was easier to pour his creative energies into something more responsive than a depressed and sick wife.

So in the midst of what looked on the outside like a very full and good life, I was feeling more and more exhausted and overwhelmed by feelings of loss. My older two sons were investigating colleges. Mother was dying. Besides my own trips to the doctor, I hadn't planned on the countless treks Amy and I were making to special tutors, speech therapists, the ophthalmologist, and the dentist. I was also feeling the unspoken pain of the loss of my ideal daughter. I had put all my emotional well-being into my husband, my children, my parents . . . and they weren't coming through for me. Nothing was turning out the way I thought it would, and life seemed too much to bear. But I was a wife and a mother—I couldn't quit.

There were times I seemed to cope—especially when we would travel somewhere, or be outside. We bought a boat and spent some time cruising around the San Juan Islands off the Washington coast. I would reason, *Maybe I am just tired. If I could just rest for a while I could get well.* But as we drove over the mountains toward home, that old familiar feeling of pain and pressure would be there. I couldn't manage the life I had created for myself.

The medication did seem to help some, but oddly enough as I look back, I never connected my emotional state to my physical condition. I just never put the two together. I was convinced no one worked as hard as I did just to be normal. Before I got sick, I'd had boundless energy to do my responsibilities and do them well: pre-pare meals, entertain, get to the kids' baseball games, teach Bible studies, write articles, and speak at women's events. But when things started falling apart, I was aware that everybody wanted something from me and I just couldn't give it anymore . . . and I felt like saying to God, "What do You want from me too? You who are standing a distance away, detached, arms folded, watching . . . but not connecting? Do I have to dance a certain way, perform well—get a smattering of applause—then do it again? (Trying, trying, trying to please You?)"

I understood exactly what author Lewis Smedes meant when he wrote, "Guilt was not my problem as I felt it. What I felt most was a glob of unworthiness that I could not tie down to any concrete sins I was guilty of. What I needed more than pardon was a sense that God accepted me, owned me, held me, affirmed me, and would never let go of me even if he was not too impressed with what he had on his hands."[1]

I kept coming back to this one thought: *Why can't I be loved just for being me?* It was a deep, primal emotion and with the question, I smothered back sobs. I kept thinking that if I could find a private altar somewhere and find God, He would hear me and hold me. I just couldn't get there. I wrote in my journal, *O God, I am desperate for Your voice, Your touch upon my life. Whom have I but You? No one. You alone know my heart and my deepest agonies. I long to live a life of focused purpose, love and goodness. Father, my life is irretrievably broken without Your touch. You must be bigger to me than my failure and my fears.*

🌿 🌿 🌿

After four years of struggling physically, I seemed to be getting worse. My face was going numb, so one day I was at the neurologist having a spinal tap. After the spinal tap, I needed to stay flat for a couple of hours, and the doctor said before he left the room, "If this lupus is going to the central nervous system, it could be fatal." With those words ringing in my ears, he left the room. I remember staring at the beige wall, feeling absolutely at the bottom, "Lord," I prayed, "why is this happening to me?" It seemed that I heard His still, small voice: *Just let go. Let go of what?* I wondered. I only knew how to grab on, to add to my life. I didn't know how to let go.

Shortly after, at my husband's urging, I went to the Mayo Clinic to get a thorough examination. After many grueling tests, I sat in Dr. O'Duffy's office. A short, wiry, Irish man with a mop of curly graying hair, he bored me through with his blue eyes. "I find no lupus.

Congratulations. You are organically and neurologically healthy."

"Thanks," I said weakly. "Then what's wrong with me?"

"I believe that stress is the cause of your pain."

I was astounded. "You mean it's *just stress?*"

"There's no such thing as 'just stress.' Stress causes, or exacerbates, most major illnesses. Your mind, body, and soul are connected. You're a package deal." He looked at my chart, describing my life. "You say you're married to a 'type A' man . . . You've got five children, trying to raise them with high standards and write a book about it. You're helping edit a magazine, you run a prison ministry, and work in the local church. You're also on the school board." He asked me frankly, "What is *wrong* with you? Who do you think you are—superwoman?" He went on, "If you want, you can have a label—fibromyalgia—and you can continue to take all these medications. Or you can do something that is harder, but in the long run, better. You can go home and confront your life to see why you have so much stress that you are in this much pain."

This was a watershed moment for me, and I knew I had been confronted by a choice. On the plane trip home, I felt broken and humbled. The question upper-most in my mind was, *Why am I, a follower of Him who said, "My yoke is easy and My burden is light," living with this much stress?* For the first time I admitted I had a prob-lem that only I could address. But where should I start?

Realizing I had a problem was an important step, and Dr. O'Duffy helped me define it. I knew my life was severely out of balance, even though I wasn't doing bad things; it was a life filled with wonderful and challenging things I thought I'd always wanted. But it was too much, and I was being crushed by it. I cringed as I remembered making a disparaging comment about someone who was struggling to find "who she was." I had laughed. "How self-absorbed!" Humbled, I realized I didn't know who I was.

"Who I was" had been so defined as "wife of Bill," "mother of Jon, Eric, Chris, Andy, and Amy," and "mag-azine editor"—roles that I loved, and I would still tell you that's all I ever really wanted—and yet I felt lost. Now as I look at family videos of that time, I look like an efficient machine, my face like a mask. Who was I, and how had I gotten to this place?

When I got home to Oregon, the first thing I did—at

Dr. O'Duffy's suggestion—was to throw away my medications. I began by reading about stress. Hans Selye in *The Stress of Life* wrote about how life is expendable. And like a bank account, if we take continual withdrawals and do not make deposits, we will be overdrawn. That was me. Over the years, I had not taken time to relax nor time to nurture my own self. I had been running in the red, emotionally and physically, for too long.

I took a stress management class, which gave me insight as to why my body was telling me as clearly as it could that things had to change. One of the most life-shaping principles I learned was that although there are some circumstances that are not possible to change, I could change the way I *framed* them. This simple insight opened my thinking, and continues to help me because my tendency was to think that if something needed to be done, I had to do it—and do it well.

About this time, our magazine was going through a redesign, something periodicals occasionally do to stay fresh. The consultant who critiqued the magazine commented, "Your magazine is good, but it's overdesigned. You have too much text and too much illustration. The text and illustrations are good, but you need more white space to set off what you want to say."

A light went on inside of me—*white space!* That's what I needed. My life was overdesigned—full of good things, but so full that it was empty. True to my personality, I craved spontaneity, but there was no time for it because there was too much to do, and not enough time to do it. Perhaps if I had been living with such a crammed-full life only a year or so, I wouldn't have crashed as I did—but I had gone this way for several years. I rarely cut myself slack. In order to get everything done, I had to do several things at once—fold clothes while talking on the phone, work in the car, read manuscripts in waiting rooms. Every minute had to count for me.

One day on my way home I got stopped in a construction line and, as usual, I had meals to prepare, correspondence to deal with, phone calls to make, dental appointments for the children, preparation for an editorial planning meeting . . . Fifteen minutes ticked by, and there I sat. I was absolutely fuming. *I did not have time for this!*

But finally I turned the car off, leaned back, and opened the sun roof. *What . . . a . . . gorgeous day!* finally filtered in. Warm sunshine and the musky smell of pine needles filled the air. The sky was blue in a blaze of glory as it can be in central Oregon. I looked up and saw a black hawk circling high, soaring effortlessly on the air currents. A vaguely familiar quote having to do with "birds of the air" and "will He not care much more for you" made itself at home in my mind.

I wondered, *Why can't I be like that bird—just be? Just enjoy God's creation? Why can't I?*

I Began to Deal with the Truth of My Life

I began in every area of my life to consciously try to bring balance. I realized I had been neglecting my physical body, and exercise now was no longer an option, it was a necessity. The first thing I did was to start walking, consistently. This continues to be one of my biggest stress-reducers, and just to get outside puts things in perspective for me. I also started going to bed at a decent hour every night. These may seem like elementary steps, but in the past, if I had a deadline or more work to do, I would try to finish no matter how late (or early the hour).

I learned that it's important to be spiritually balanced

as well as physically and emotionally balanced, so even in my reading I began to read some fiction and history, balancing out the heavier theological and deeper spiritual reading. Years ago a neighbor commented to me somewhat wistfully, "You're always dressed up and you're always going to church." As I look back, I know I didn't have time to just have coffee and be her friend. I was too busy "doing" spirituality.

As I pondered what needed to change in my life, a question that helped me was, "When am I most fully alive?" I realized that I was crowding out a very important part of myself—the love of beauty, of music; time to be creative, to develop deeper, better relationships; time to just think, to reflect. I dug out my old Chopin and Bach and began playing again—just for my own enjoyment. I began memorizing a few good lines of poetry for the sheer pleasure of the words.

I Needed to Carry Only My Burden

It was a lot of work dealing with all of this, but I stubbornly persisted. More than anything, I wanted to be an effective wife and mother and friend, and for that to happen, I knew I had to change. I realized I was carrying more than my share, albeit self-appointed. For instance, I asked the family for more help around the house. It was not so much the physical work that was smothering me—although it was considerable—but it was the worry and anxiety that I had internalized that was taking its toll. I worried over Amy (how could I help her?); I worried over our four sons (would they make good choices?); I worried about Bill's weight. I had to realize it was all right to be concerned and to pray, but I had to come to the point where I saw there is a God, and I was not it! It is lonely to claim responsibility for one's self, but it is right. I had to let go of trying to control.

I Needed to Ask for Help

> The longest journey is the journey inward.
> —Dag Hammarskjold, *Markings*[2]

I swallowed my pride and decided to talk to a counselor who could give me insight and perspective I wouldn't get anywhere else. This was a terrifying step for me because it confronted my pride as I took time to honestly ask, *Why do I drive myself so? What am I trying to prove?* I learned that early imprintations are powerful. I grew up singing about grace, but I didn't live it—works and performance were the way to acceptance.

And of course my own works weren't good enough. They looked back at me, accusing: *You've neglected nutrition . . . discipline for the kids . . . helping the children read better. You need to clean closets. The refrigerator is awful. You could have written that article better. You've neglected your own body, exercise, diet. You're way behind on your correspondence; now they will suspect what is only true—you're unreliable and incompetent. You could have done better with that project.* The inner comments were subtle but constant—not great, earth-shaking thoughts—just the small but consistent threads woven throughout my life that much was hanging on my shoulders and I was not keeping up.

A major reason for my depression I'm convinced was due to my twisted view of God—that He was a remote, mysterious deity and that I had to work constantly to try to gain His approval. The voice of the taskmaster, "Do more, pray more, do it better," was not God's voice.

These were difficult voices to contend with, because it seemed they were pushing me to do good things. How could good things be bad? To counteract these thoughts, I began memorizing verses about grace, often seeing them for the first time. *By grace am I saved through faith— not of works, lest I boast.* Grace means *not* of myself. It is God's gift. *Gift.* No strings. Accepted into the beloved, just as I am.

It was in the counseling sessions that I realized I was a perfectionist—a spiritual perfectionist—and that I was heaping condemnation on myself and suffering greatly. Excellence is a quality that should be rewarded, but it's impossible to reach perfection, and when my humanity would inevitably reveal itself, the voice of condemnation would begin hammering me. It is astounding to think how we can be wounded by life and then adopt those very wounds as our way of living.

I wrote in my journal, *God, how I need a fresh baptism of Your love and grace. Help me put away childish things. I don't want to be a little girl performing to be noticed. By grace I am saved. O God, help me to look into my children's eyes, their faces, and love them not for what they do, but for who they are.*

Dealing with the Work of My Life

It was not easy for me to think in fresh patterns, to frame my thoughts in positive ways . . . to live in grace and simply give myself a break. It was not easy, trying to escape the desert. How did I get to this place? Of course part of it was through legalistic thinking, and also a lot of it was by just living life in our fast-paced world—working too hard, not stopping to take time to do the things I was created and gifted to do and be. I was tortured by feeling that I never had enough time—not even time to grieve when my father died. I didn't take the time to respect my heavy burden of just caring for a family and a daughter with special needs. I didn't take time to care for my physical self, and many of my problems came from being physically ill.

There were times when I wanted to give up, and my old vulnerability—to earn acceptance—seemed easier than a life of grace. I had to contend for grace, as the writer of Hebrews describes as making "every effort to enter that rest" (Heb. 4:11 NIV). I am grateful that Bill supported my counseling and efforts to honestly confront my life. I didn't know much—but I knew that Bill loved me and was committed to me and our family and I loved him. I just hung on to the little that I knew.

Hearing God's Voice

Not long after I returned from the Mayo Clinic, I took a walk on a fall day to a hidden lake not far from our home. Since there are no roads there, I walked on a trail. The sky was deep blue, the lake rimmed by aspen trees turning yellow. The reflection of the trees on the lake was so clear it was almost like a double picture. *Be like this,* it seemed God was saying to me. *When you are still before Me, you can then reflect Me.*

"Yes, I want that," I responded, but inside my heart was torn. I protested, "What's wrong with a creek running through the meadow? A river? It gets more places, sees more things. God, You know I like to be involved, busy."

But creeks don't reflect. They're not deep. Still waters are deep. You knew this place was here, didn't you? You sought it out because of the restorative nature of it. When you are still before Me, people who are thirsty will seek you out to learn of Me.

Why did I resist the stillness so? I think it was because that is where I had to listen to the pain that I was so creative at avoiding and look at my less-than-perfect life, look at my disappointments and grieve my losses. I was afraid of the stillness because I didn't want to admit that my attempts at perfection were to mask the pain inside— which is exactly where God wanted to pour His love and grace. The poet W. H. Auden wrote, "It is where we are wounded that God speaks to us."

The overwhelming conviction that I didn't want to live anymore was absolutely right—I could not continue to live that way. I began doing something I had never considered important—and that was to protect myself by establishing and respecting boundaries.

I relinquished some administrative responsibilities that were draining me. It was time for me to stop reading other people's manuscripts and write my own. It was a matter of saying no to some things in order to say yes to what I was supposed to do. This principle sounds like such a cliché, yet for me it was new. I was beginning to understand that I was the gatekeeper of my life—no one else would answer to God for my own life but me.

I tentatively began keeping a quiet time in the morning with Scripture and journaling, trying to make choices out of waiting on God and listening for His still, small voice. I learned to be still—still in my spirit—a sense of waiting on God and journaling honest prayers as I studied Scripture. I had been afraid of being honest, because my thoughts at times were so dark. I identified with writer Anne LaMott: "My mind remains a bad neighborhood that I don't like to go into alone." But paradoxically, solitude and honest journaling combined with the discipline of Scripture, and prayer became a catharsis and brought insights that opened up my thinking.

During this time, my mother died. I wrote in my journal,

Mother died three weeks ago.

I write that line but it is still so hard to believe. How can she die? That woman of laughter, of music? Of poetry and quick wit—unfailing arms of love and acceptance? Even in her declining state, she loved. How can we say it is better for her? She is gone! Gone from us. But present to God, to loved ones on the other side. Surely it must be so. Death cannot still one so vibrant, so lovely. I keep trying to burn the memory of her laughter, the sound of her voice, the warmth of her smile deep into my mind so I won't forget. How does one grieve *and* live? Laugh *and* cry?

Her death was a huge loss for me, and yet I'm grateful that I was learning the eloquent lessons of the desert—to be honest about the pain, to grieve when it's time. Because I'd always rightly believed I'd been given much, I felt guilty about acknowledging loss. The desert forced me to pay attention, and I've learned that seeing the loss does not diminish the blessings; indeed, it enhances it.

There are three extremely important principles I learned in my desert experience that I am passionate about sharing, and the sequence is important.

1. It is important to honestly acknowledge personal pain, disappointment, or defeat.
2. It is essential to relinquish it to God and receive His grace, comfort, and forgiveness.
3. Freedom comes when I choose an attitude of gratefulness and thanksgiving to God in the situation.

Praising God in the midst of difficult things is tremendously liberating and dramatically changes the whole picture. As I began thanking God for my daughter, Amy, I began to see a delightful person—what a valiant little soul she is, with a great heart of compassion. She has a sense of humor, and although she still can be explosive, she deals with her learning disabilities with grace and effort. She's now a senior in high school, and remarkably, Amy loves her rather frenetic mother almost as much as I love her. *Amy is a gift.* What changed? Not Amy. The situation changed because I began to see her as a gift.

I live near a high desert and often have to drive through it. I am quite frankly repelled by the desert. It's arid, flat. Nothing seems to grow there. And yet the desert is a powerful place to be because that is where life is stripped of its distractions. In Scripture, it was in the desert where God prepared Moses for his great calling of leading the children of Israel. It was in the wilderness where God first comforted and fed Elijah, and then gave him his further marching orders. John the Baptist preached from the desert, and Jesus was tempted in the desert before He began His earthly ministry.

The desert taught me that life is not to be lived around the edges—the periphery. It's easy to be caught up in projects, calendars, doctrine . . . instead of things that touch us most deeply: our feelings and emotions and loves and fears. The desert forced me to do that—to be honest about what was inside of me. It is powerful stuff, after all, and affects the rest of life. How amazing that God does speak to us—but it takes courage and willingness to listen.

I've learned that the desert itself is not a tragedy. The tragedy would be not to hear what God was saying to me there. As I was confronted by what I viewed as the mess of my life, I knew God's comfort and provision as never before. In my weakness, He became my strength. In my emptiness and confusion, He became my Rock and purpose for living.

Meditating on Scripture and studying it to get an accurate picture of God became all-important to me. After all, we are vulnerable to other voices in the desert as well. Satan came to Jesus in the desert, urging Him to turn the stones into bread. I found it was critical that I learn to know God's voice by studying Scripture during this time.

Reflections Later

I never want to forget the lessons of the desert, although the desert speaks "death" in a way. Yet out of death comes life, because Jesus said that in order to live we must die. I've learned to treasure the truth, to allow the truth of life *in*. Losses happen. Death separates loved ones. Illness may come. There are no perfect children or perfect marriages.

Yet the astounding, wonderful surprise of God's grace and redemption is an overwhelming truth. And if there is anything I know about God from reading Scripture, it is that He is the Redeemer, and in His time He redeems all things that we place in His hands.

How is my life now? I am well, physically. My life is still very busy, and my list of things to do never seems to get completely checked off. The temptation to accept inward pressure never ends as life offers a continuing menu of change.

What the experience has deeply changed for me is that I've learned it's enough for me to only give what I have. And what I have to give is me, in all my weakness and humanity, leaning hard on Jesus. I basically just show up—which is enough! I try to live in the moment and savor the simple things of life that are so profound. Late this afternoon I stopped to see a breathtaking view of the setting sun behind the clouds and snow-covered mountains. I breathed in the beauty and said "Thank You" to God. I never want to lose the wonder of the beauty of God's world.

I've learned to thank God for the people and situations He's placed in my life, knowing they are gifts from Him. I've learned to be kinder to myself, more protective from the crush of life. I'm learning to be more courageous and truthful in my expressions. I've also learned that the mind-body connection is powerful. I was getting a strong wake-up call from my body to pay attention. We are fearfully and wonderfully made, and God speaks to us through our pain, both physical and emotional.

The psalmist said, "Behold, You desire truth in the inward parts, / And in the hidden part You will make me to know wisdom" (Ps. 51:6 NKJV). The inward part—the covered-up part, the real me that struggled so and indeed still struggles at times—is the part where, if I have the courage to pay attention and ask God, I truly learn wisdom.

The desert experience also gave me a sense of humility and compassion. Now I have greater empathy and understanding for others. Henri Nouwen asked this poignant question: "'Who can take away suffering without entering into it?' The great illusion of leadership is to think that others can be led out of the desert by someone who has never been there."[3]

I have learned to set my hope in God. I would have said all along that that was where my hope was, but in truth it was not. It was in what I could *do*. I have learned to say, "My hope is in You, Lord!"

> He turns a wilderness into pools of water,
> And dry land into watersprings.
> There He makes the hungry dwell,
> That they may establish a city for a dwelling place,
> And sow fields and plant vineyards,
> That they may yield a fruitful harvest. (Ps. 107:35–37 NKJV)

chapter 4

Extreme Disappointment

Gordon MacDonald

❦ ONCE, AT A MUCH YOUNGER MOMENT IN MY LIFE, the search committee of a Christian organization of no small repute asked if I would be a candidate to become their president. My first reaction was one of astonishment. I felt honored, quite inadequate, and challenged all at the same time. I said yes, I would be glad to enter into discussions with them.

Soon I was aware that many others across the world had been similarly approached, and I concluded that my name would quickly disappear from the committee's list. There were too many worthy people under consideration. I was not in their league.

But while other names did disappear from that list, mine did not. And after some months there came a day when only two people seemed to have survived this rather thorough selection process. I was one of them. Suddenly, my wife, Gail, and I knew that we were involved in something quite serious and there was a chance that I would be called upon to assume a heavy responsibility that was probably well beyond both my experience and ability. Only a God who revels in calling obscure, sometimes weak, and very flawed people (like Gideon, Simon Peter, and Saul of Tarsus) to giant tasks could arrange a scenario like this, I thought. And that notion kept me going and helped me to make sense of what was happening.

Several weeks before the final decision between the two candidates was to be made, Gail and I withdrew into a kind of seclusion. We gave ourselves to prayer and contemplation of God's purpose in this matter. We knew that I had not sought this task and did not feel humanly adequate for it. Furthermore, we could not imagine what it might take out of us in terms of energy and spirit, how it might test our health and our marriage. We talked for hours, wept more than once, laughed at the absurdity that such a thing might come to pass. But, and this was the bottom line, if this was what God was asking, we would be obedient. That was how I'd been taught, and that was how I'd chosen to live.

Those weeks of quiet were among the most powerful; the most blessed contemplative times in my life.
Every time we turned around, we seemed to be confronted with indications (signs, hints, even what some
would call "words of knowledge") that when the committee made its final decision, I would be asked to take
on this job of demanding leadership. Neither of us is a
seeker after signs, and we are not pushovers for "messages" that claim to be direct communications from
heaven; that has not been characteristic of our journey
of faith. Nevertheless, in our reading, in the communications we received from trusted friends and counselors,
in the depths of our souls, a conviction seemed to
become clear: God was preparing us for something that
would irrevocably alter our lives. I remember thinking
that this must be something of what Moses experienced
out in the desert as the God of his fathers spoke to him
so certainly out of a nondescript bush.

Then came decision day. It followed hard on the heels
of hours and hours of discussions and interviews. And
my heart became increasingly more convinced. I would
be asked to do this job.

But I was wrong! In an instant, this blessed process, this

marvelous desert experience in which I'd sought God's purposes and He'd seemed to answer so powerfully, came to a brutal and abrupt end. The committee's chairman phoned to say that they had picked the other person.

My reaction was calm and unprotesting. I knew that they had made a good and right choice. The other man was clearly the better, the more qualified of the two of us, and with his selection the organization's future lay in highly competent hands.

But what I did not realize was that another desert experience had just begun. That I was moving from a state of high confidence to one of total inner confusion, utter despair. For the question began to erupt out of the deeper parts of my life: What have those weeks and months been about? How could I have been so sure that I'd heard God's voice and been so wrong? I dared to begin to ask why God had made such a total fool out of me. Result: I lost all certainty that I knew how to hear God's word at all. In fact, I reached a moment when I wondered if God had ever spoken at all. Perhaps the stories behind the call of Moses, Jeremiah, and Saul of Tarsus were merely tales from fertile imaginations.

I cannot exaggerate the awfulness of this moment.

Nor can I describe the inner anguish that went on for more than a year. In fact, the effects lingered deep within for several years. The issue was simple: I felt as if I had surrendered everything into the hands of God, that I had been prompted (again, by my own wishes) to believe that He was expressing His sovereign will, that all of heaven had been behind this. I have never felt so totally led in the holy way. And never had I been so wrong! I cannot exaggerate how shaken I was.

In the aftermath of that enormous personal disillusionment, I found that virtually every private prayer was automatically prefaced with words to this effect: "God, forgive me if I tell You that I no longer know Your language. I feel misled, let down, unsure that You do indeed speak with any clarity." Sometimes these words were less respectful. Rather, they were bitter and even vindictive.

While my public activity of ministry continued in preaching, praying, and leading a congregation, my inner life fell into disarray. I was only beginning to learn the significance of the words of the psalmist that were later echoed by a suffering Christ: "Why have You forsaken Me?"

Some have said that such a disillusioning experience is

necessary for any saint-in-the-making. They've said that one's desert experience must include a time when all sense of assurance is shattered in order that we might know that the thoughts of God are not our thoughts. Some suggest that we have to become fools at certain points so that we will never fully presume that we have gotten God figured out and that we can predict His ways. Are they correct when they observe that God will do anything to point us in the direction of humility? Anything?

If that is the case, I have learned the lesson well in my own desert. It took years for me to lay that difficult experience to rest. On a practical basis, I have never questioned the conclusion of the matter. Had I been asked to accept that responsibility I would have failed at the job, and my insufficiency would have been damaging to that organization. But why God took me through the process and appeared to dangle the possibilities out in front of me in such a tantalizing fashion remains something of a mystery. I shall ask Him about it someday . . . or perhaps in that glorious moment I will not care.

This bit of personal history is a mystery with which I am now comfortable. And thankful. And settled. And what have I learned from that visit to the desert?

1. Never be seduced by bigness, by fancy processes, by the siren call of notoriety, by little games that purport to pave the way to a great God.

2. Never simplify the process by which God leads men and women.

3. Never presume that the way of the cross is not paved with moments of disappointment and disillusionment, which build character, resilience, and awe.

chapter 5

In the Face of Death

John C. Maxwell

🍃 LET'S GO BACK TO DECEMBER 18, 1998, AND AN experience that came out of the blue—one I'll never forget. On December 18 our INJOY organization, which is located in Atlanta, Georgia, was having its Christmas party. The Christmas party is special because all the members of our team come home for the holidays, and we are all able to be together. We had the most wonderful evening.

As the party was coming to an end, I began to feel sick to my stomach and needed some fresh air but never really thought much of it until I was hugging the people good-bye. Connie and her husband, Ron, a couple who work with us, came over and gave me a big hug. As she touched the hair behind my neck she said, "Your neck is cold and breaking out in sweat." I put my hand back there and realized immediately that something was wrong. I sat down and they went over to tell my wife, Margaret. I'm not one to be sick at all; I've been very blessed with good health, but as soon as Margaret saw me she said, "Call 911!" I lay down on the floor and people came around me, about forty to fifty people. They gave me some room and were doing the things they were supposed to do in such a situation—rubbing my hands, giving me air, taking my shoes off, and waiting for the ambulance to arrive. I was starting to have chest pains at this time and realized I was having a heart attack; I knew that I was really in trouble.

The ambulance arrived and took me to the nearest hospital. When I arrived they said there was no problem, that I was having a heart attack but that they had gotten to it early and they would be able to stabilize me. I felt very relaxed and believed that they would.

I wasn't frightened at this time but felt a sense that God's hand was on me, and I knew by the words spoken to me that they were going to be able to help me. They began to work on me and gave me some medication to try to stabilize the heart, but it wasn't stabilizing—the chest pains were just as intense and continued for a long period of time.

The doctors allowed my wife, Margaret, to come in. Initially everyone had been speaking positively, but after an hour and a half they were beginning to tell her not to be too hopeful, that this was a pretty serious thing. They were implying to her that I might not make it—that they could not get my heart stabilized.

Many people from INJOY had already gone home from the Christmas party before anyone realized I was having a heart attack. This included my assistant, Linda Eggers, and her husband, Patrick. They were called and were on their way to the hospital when she said to Patrick, "Let me stop by the office and pick up my Rolodex; I may need it tonight." This was of God. She picked up the Rolodex and went to the hospital waiting room where the rest of the INJOY people were waiting. Margaret told her that things were not looking good for me. They started going through the Rolodex and came to the name of Dr. John Bright Cage and immediately Margaret and Linda agreed they needed to call him.

I would like to pause for a moment to talk about how God places His hand upon His people. What's so awesome is that six months prior to this heart attack, I was having a luncheon meeting in Nashville with several people from my publisher, Thomas Nelson, including Sam Moore, Rolf Zettersten, and Dr. John Bright Cage, whom I had not met until this time. Dr. Cage had helped Sam Moore with some heart problems. When Sam asked John Bright, "Is there anything I can do for you?" John Bright said, "Yes, I'd like to meet one of your authors" and mentioned that he'd like to meet me. So it was at this luncheon that I met Dr. Cage for the first time. In our conversation that day, Dr. Cage shared with me that he felt that God had called him to watch after my health, and to be honest, very foolishly I kind of blew it off. I told him that I was in good health, that I get physicals every year, etc. But I'll never forget this: Dr. Cage leaned over the table and said more intently to me, "No, you're not in as good health as you think. You're overweight. I get your schedule, and I see that you're working too hard, you travel too much, and you're a candidate for a heart attack." Of course, this is his field. But what touched my heart is that he gave me his card and said, "I really want to help you. I want you to call me day or night."

Little did I realize that when he gave me his card with his phone number and said to call him day or night that we would be doing that very thing, for it was about 1:00 A.M. when Linda called him. The question is, What led Dr. Cage to say what he did six months prior to my heart attack? This is a story of how God keeps the links of a chain together regardless of what we know at any point in time in our life. I'm convinced that God had a divine plan for me and that Dr. Cage was a link in that chain.

In retrospect, there were so many variables that only God could have had His hand in it. Linda, my assistant, called Dr. Cage about 1:00 A.M., explaining to him that I was in trouble, that we had moved to Atlanta only about one year previously and did not know any cardiologists or doctors in the area, and asked him if there was anything he could do. He asked for Linda's cell phone number and agreed to call back in five minutes with assistance.

Before we go further, let's back up to look at the chain of events to show how God had His plan in this. When Dr. Cage was an intern-in-residence he would drive home in the evening around 6:00 or 6:30 P.M., and listen to WNAZ in Nashville, which carried my broadcast at that time. So during his entire internship and residency he would listen to my program on his way home if he wasn't on call. In 1994 I announced for the first time that Promise Keepers was going to have regional conferences outside of Colorado and the closest one was going to be Indianapolis. Immediately Dr. Cage and a friend signed up and drove to Indianapolis. I was the speaker at the Promise Keepers' Indianapolis meeting and had the topic of "Leave Your Jacket"; the most important part of the speech was about what the definition of success was, and Dr. Cage said it stuck to his heart. The message was basically that it's not important that I have INJOY or that Dr. Dobson has Focus on the Family; the most important thing we have is our family, and that we have their honor and respect because of what we've done for them. If people who are closest to us do not love and respect us most, then something is wrong with us.

Back to my story: I was hanging between life and death when the call went out to Dr. Cage. He had doctor friends in Atlanta who were intervention cardiologists and, knowing this was what I needed, called a friend who was a cardiologist at Emory. Dr. Cage expressed the urgency of my need, and his friend, Dr. Marshall, came immediately to my bedside. He called an ambulance to take me to a catheterization lab at another nearby hospital so that the blocked artery could be opened. He met the ambulance, took me immediately to the cath lab, and removed the blockage.

Because of that, I do not have any damage to my heart now. I am a very fortunate and grateful man! I'm overwhelmed at the goodness of God. The world would look at something like this and say it was a coincidence, but it wasn't; it was an act of God. I believe in the sovereignty of God. Dr. Cage so beautifully helped us out in this process, and Dr. Marshall is now my heart doctor in Atlanta. We have developed a great relationship.

I don't understand why God spared my life when others have died. I feel I have a great responsibility now, that I need to get about my calling and do what God has called me to do with great intensity and not take for granted my health or my calling. You cannot look face-to-face with death like that and not be changed. Priorities need to be reexamined. I've always had a passion for the Lord, and I've always had a passion for pastors.

However, two things are new in my life now.

Number one is that no matter how much you tell people you love them, no matter how much you express this love, it is never enough. In other words, as I lay there in the emergency room I wanted one more time to tell Margaret how much I loved her, that I loved being her husband, and I wanted to tell my kids that I loved being their dad. You just can't tell the people you love that you love them enough, so I want to tell you that no matter how great that relationship is—never take it for granted.

The second thing I've learned is not to take life for granted. I did enjoy life, but I also took it for granted. I just assumed that my ministry would be fulfilled over a span of so many years, but now I don't assume that. Every day I get up and I tell God how grateful I am for life, that Margaret is my wife and best friend, that my kids are healthy, that my ministry is where I think it should be. When I was on that table the warmth of God and the greatness of God just overwhelmed me. It was the first time I had actually stared death in the face, yet God gave me peace and I realized that He loved me unconditionally. His grace just overwhelmed me, and the witness of the Spirit that I was a child of

God removed the fear factor, regardless of the outcome. I can say that God was there to minister to me in a wonderful way.

Before I could talk about my heart attack publicly, I felt I needed a year to go by so that I could have integrity in the things I wanted to talk about. Everyone knows what it's like to have something traumatic happen to him or her and then immediately make a major decision. You'll say, "I'm never going to do this again" or "I'm always going to do that." I've done that hundreds of times but wish I hadn't. Do you connect with this? But as I lay in that hospital bed I realized I was way too close to the trauma to find out if those decisions I was trying to make in that hospital bed would become reality.

So I've waited for a year. I remember a lot of cards, letters, phone calls, etc., during those first few months, and on a couple of occasions Dr. Jim Dobson called me to see how I was doing. One day we were talking on the phone and he said, "John, when are you going to talk about this publicly?" I told him I was going to wait a year. He has also had a heart attack and a major physical setback. He said, "Don't wait that long. You'll lose the emotion." I told him, "The reason I want to wait that long is that I'm not sure I can back up the decisions I'm making. I'm not sure I have the character and the discipline to back up what I really feel right now." So he talked me into coming on *Focus on the Family* where I shared the heart attack story in detail. The experience of being on this program with Dr. Dobson helped me to sort through all of those conflicting emotions.

Now, one year later, I have a great desire to get the lessons I've learned to others. I have a great desire that those who read this and need to make changes *will* make those changes. This is where my greatest joy is going to be—that others will begin to take a self-inventory and make transitions in their lives that will help them run the course for the long haul.

We're not running the Christian life like a hundred-yard dash but as a race for the whole term of our lives. Jim Roan said, "Don't let your learning be only knowledge; let your learning lead to action." I think one of the biggest difficulties in our lives is that what we learn is kept only as head knowledge and therefore never changes our lives. Howie Hendricks, a wonderful friend and mentor of mine who has taught me so much through his books and his lectures, said, "Learning is change." Howie would say, "If you haven't changed, you haven't learned. Just because you can put it on paper or because you can recite it doesn't mean it's yours. It's not yours until you change."

After I had gone through the worst of my ordeal, the day finally came when I was going to be released from the hospital and allowed to go home. I had kept a legal pad close to me in the hospital bed where I had written down questions I wanted to ask the doctor before I left. I had a pretty long list. The main question at the very top of that list of all the stuff I was going to ask him was, "Can I live a long life?" There I was, fifty-one years of age, having a heart attack, and I wanted to know if I had a short time or a long time to look forward to. Could I look forward to being eighty-five? Could I have a long, fulfilling life? That was the big question.

I'll never forget when Dr. Marshall was the doctor who came in the room that day and I led off with the most important question: "Can I live a long life?" He looked at me and said, "Yes, but to do that you will have to make some major changes." Obviously, my next question was, "What would those major changes have to be?" As he told me what those changes were, I realized the future years would have to be completely different from the first fifty-one years of my life. So I asked myself, "Can I honestly make these changes?"

I asked myself that day in the hospital room, "Can I change?" My answer to you today is, Yes, I can—with integrity.

Another question then was, "Can I have a quality of life?" The answer is, Yes, I can.

I asked, "Can I continue in my ministry?" The answer to you today is, Yes, I can.

The next question was, "Are my best days behind me or ahead of me?" The answer today is, The best days are ahead of me.

When I learned what changes I needed to make, I said to myself, "With God's help I will do it," and here I am, eighteen months later, living a new lifestyle. It's not been easy, but with God's help I'm feeling blessed.

Out of my "desert experience" I've learned a few things:

- God's hand is on my life.
- You can never tell family and friends too much that you love them.

- Prayer is the most important thing.
- Be grateful to God for everything.

chapter *6*

Formed in the Wilderness

J. I. Packer

IN RECENT YEARS IN OUR WESTERN WORLD, MUCH interest has been shown in the cultivating of spiritual life (*spirituality,* as it is called), both among Christians, for whom spiritual life means communing with God in Christ through the Holy Spirit, and among others for whom spiritual life means simply exploring one's self-hood and seeking to maintain it intact against external pressures. Since one main trigger for these discussions has been the sense that in our big cities we are squeezed out of shape, it is no wonder that an image of the desert as a place where one gets away from it all, lives simply, and has room to move often arises with a rosy glow when spirituality is debated.

Raw material for establishing the excellence of the desert is drawn from both Christian and non-Christian sources. Christian sources include Origen's view of Israel's wilderness wanderings as a type of each believer's pilgrimage; early monastic asceticism, which centered on living away from the city and practicing poverty, celibacy, bodily hardship, and sustained prayer; the familiar routine of periodic retreats into solitude to refocus one's desire for God and straighten out one's soul; and much devotional wisdom from the monasteries, where for the past sixteen centuries life has been lived somewhat out of the world. Raw material from non-Christian sources comes from various forms of depth psychology: Eastern meditative techniques for isolating the self from the world and detaching it from the body; proposals for self-realization and self-care; and the agonized consciousness of many contemporary artists.

The desert discussions themselves tend to be self-absorbed, sentimental, and confused, a far cry from God's agenda for the desert as seen in the examples from the Bible that we will be examining. But it is God's agenda that should concern us, and when we discuss spiritual life, and desert experiences as one aspect of it, God's agenda should give direction and set limits to what we say.

So it is important first to examine the divine purpose of the desert. What agenda does God have in leading His people into desert experiences? Paul declared that "God causes all things to work together for good to those who love God, to those who are called according to His purpose" (Rom. 8:28 NASB). The good referred to is to be understood in terms not of ease and comfort as such, but of the fulfillment of the goal stated by Paul in Ephesians 5:25–27, both for the church as a body and for every Christian as part of it: "Christ . . . loved the church and gave Himself up for her; that He might sanctify her, having cleansed her . . . that He might present to Himself the church in all her glory, having no spot or wrinkle or any such thing; but that she should be holy and blameless" (NASB).

What does that imply? One thing it certainly implies is that when in God's providence believers are exposed to the pressures of being isolated, opposed, tempted, humbled, disappointed, and hurt, the divine purpose is that these things should further our transformation into the likeness of our Savior, and that through maintaining faith, hope, worship, and fidelity in face of these trials we should become stronger and more clearheaded than before. "Stronger" here means better able to cope with such pressures the next time they arise, and "more clear-headed" means more fully aware of two things: (1) that our love-relationship to the Father, the Son, and the Spirit matters more, and brings more joy, than any of the pleasant things—health, wealth, comfort, companions, recognition, respect, or whatever—of which we are for the present deprived; and (2) that God's plan for turning us out Jesus-like involves putting us through many disciplinary experiences that are mysterious and ungratifying to us at the time.

> We had earthly fathers to discipline us, and we respected them; shall we not much rather be subject to the Father of [our] spirits, and live? . . . He disciplines us for our good, that we may share His holiness. All discipline for the moment seems not to be joyful, but sorrowful; yet to those who have been trained by it, afterwards it yields the peaceful fruit of righteousness. (Heb. 12:9–11 NASB)

To be fanciful: if the hunk of stone out of which Michelangelo was hammering and chiseling his David could have spoken, it would no doubt have said it did not know in what shape it was going to end up; it only knew that what was currently happening was painful. And to be realistic, that is often all we are able to say when God is using griefs and pains to sculpt our souls. Perhaps we never become at all aware, and certainly we never become fully aware, of how these experiences mature and refine and at the deepest level, integrate us for our future destiny as we humbly accept and endure them. Many, however, who have had to say with the psalmist, "I have been stricken all day long, / And chastened every morning," have found themselves, like him, becoming newly and dazzlingly aware that

> I am continually with Thee;
> Thou hast taken hold of my right hand.
> With Thy counsel Thou wilt guide me,
> And afterward receive me to glory.
> Whom have I in heaven but Thee?
> And besides Thee, I desire nothing on earth.
> My flesh and my heart may fail,
> But God is the strength of my heart
>   and my portion forever. (Ps. 73:14, 23–26 NASB)

As for what Shakespeare called "the slings and arrows of outrageous fortune"—the devastating disasters that seem to strike at random, without rhyme or reason, and to multiply far more in some lives than in others—the believer's proper confidence about their place in God's plan is well reflected in the words of promise, drawn from Scripture, that the old hymn puts into God's mouth:

> When through the deep waters I cause thee to go,
> The rivers of grief shall not thee overflow;
> For I will be with thee, thy troubles to bless,
> And sanctify to thee thy deepest distress.
>
> When through fiery trials thy pathway shall lie,
> My grace all-sufficient shall be thy supply;
> The flame shall not hurt thee; I only design
> Thy dross to consume, and thy gold to refine.

The desert, or wilderness, appears in Scripture not just as a place where certain things happened, but as a symbol of isolation in some form—isolation, however, into which God Himself leads us for purposes of discipline and discovery within His love-relation to us. In the desert God will discipline us for the maturing of our faith and character as disciples, and we accept the discipline because we know that spiritual advance is what it will lead to. In the desert, too, God will uncover, and show us, what we are made of spiritually, for it is a place of testing; we shall learn more than we previously knew about our present shortcomings (lovelessness, thoughtlessness, instability, indiscipline, self-absorption, malice, pride, unbelief, disordered desires, and, as the travel brochures say, much, much more); also, through God's revelatory action, we shall learn, or relearn, much about Him that calls for trust and love and praise (the greatness of His grace, His all-sufficiency, His wisdom and beauty, His faithfulness, His purpose and priorities, and so forth). The desert experience may thus have great significance in our personal pilgrimage.

Three Bible stories of desert experiences highlight these very lessons.

Story one is of the original desert journey—a forty-year journey, as it turned out to be—that began with Israel's crossing of the Red Sea to escape from Egypt and ended with Israel's crossing of Jordan to enter the promised land. The events during those years of wandering in the wilderness by which God tested His unruly people, revealed His holy character to them, drilled them in worship and discipleship, and taught them due dependence on His wisdom and power, are more than we can go over here; but this is how, in one of his final speeches, Moses summed the matter up:

> You shall remember all the way which the LORD your God has led you in the wilderness these forty years, that He might humble you, testing you, to know what was in your heart, whether you would keep His commandments or not. And He humbled you and let you be hungry, and fed you with manna . . . that He might make you understand that man does not live by bread alone, but man lives by everything that proceeds out of the mouth of the LORD . . .
>
> The LORD your God was disciplining you just as a man disciplines his son . . . He led you through the great and terrible wilderness, with its fiery serpents and scorpions and thirsty ground where there was no water; He brought water for you out of the rock of

flint . . . You shall remember the LORD your God, for it is He who is giving you power to make wealth. (Deut. 8:2–3, 5, 15, 18 NASB)

Story two is in 1 Kings 19. It tells how, following triumph over the prophets of Baal at Mount Carmel, Elijah panicked at Jezebel's threats, fled into the desert in depression and despair, wanting only to die, and was given a fresh, energizing realization of God's love and care and wisdom and power, plus a renewed commission, with new instructions, for his own continuing prophetic ministry.

Story three, found in Matthew 4:1–11 and Luke 4:1–13, tells how, immediately after His baptism and full of the Holy Spirit, Jesus "was led about by the Spirit in the wilderness for forty days, being tempted by the devil." It shows Him tempted in three different ways to be false to His calling as Son of God—that is, as the divine Messiah, God in the flesh, who came to minister to sinners in the Spirit's power and to save them by taking their place on the cross. We see Jesus triumphing over Satan's three attempts to deflect Him from the Father's will, as once he deflected Adam and Eve.

These three stories show us what essentially happens in "desert experiences." Systematic theology tells us what they mean in terms of God's gracious purposes, but only as we brood on the stories themselves, opening our hearts to their impact, using our God-given powers of empathy and imagination to identify with the characters, and begging light from the Holy Spirit—the author and interpreter of Scripture—as we go along, shall we appreciate the blend of revelation and realization, humbling and exalting, conflict and comfort that "desert experiences" bring.

But am I saying these things only from an academic point of view? Do I know what I am talking about when I speak of the desert experience? Perhaps; you shall judge. Here is a slice of my own experience that I would like to share.

It never occurred to me until now to think of what happened twenty-five years ago as a desert experience. After all, it did not involve clinical depression or relational traumas, agonies of abandonment or loss of sleep, or anything of that sort. My wife suspects that because of damage done in my childhood, suppressing distressed feelings has become instinctive to me, and she may be right. But all I know is that I can handle the negative reactions of others without too much upset inside. In this case, however, the negative reactions were less to my person than to my purposes, and it is always burdensome when one feels oneself trustee for a God-given vision that puts one out of step with former friends.

I had in my mind (perhaps that should be, heart) a vision of evangelical quickening in England, my native country, through theological education, spiritual formation, pastoral enrichment, profounder preaching, wiser evangelism, functional Christian unity, and every-member-ministry in local congregations—a vision generated and sustained by the type of pure biblical theology to which some give the name of Puritan Calvinism. Put like that, I admit, it sounds grandiose to a fault, and though I retain my hold on this vision—or, rather, it retains its hold on me—I am not at present concerned to defend it against its critics. I simply state that after fifteen years of promoting it came five years during which, through what people with other visions did in perfectly good faith to block more or less directly the things I was after, I lost all that the vision had dictated. I found myself marginalized, isolated, and required to work at unfulfilling and, I thought, flawed agendas, in a manner that made me think of the Israelites having to make bricks for Pharaoh. My life was full of business, but I had no confidence that it was all the right business, and for political reasons I was not free to say what I thought or to mark out a better way. Such was my time in the desert. Outwardly appreciated by some as a useful Christian performer, I was living like Moses in Midian, with frustration in my heart, wondering what God—whom I thought had given the vision in the first place—could possibly be up to.

Certain values were highlighted for me during those years. God alone knows how far I managed to live them out; here I merely record that He hammered them in:

1. *Goodwill.* I should not get bitter or lapse into self-pity or spend any time complaining and angling for sympathy. God was using my ministry, and I was forbidden to get fixated on my frustrations.

2. *Hope.* I was not to become cynical or apathetic about the vision I had been given or to abandon it because there was no immediate way of advancing it. God is never in a hurry, and waiting in hope is a biblical discipline.

3. *Faithfulness.* As a husband, father, teacher, honorary assistant clergyman, and occasional author, I had plenty each day to get on with, and I could not honor God by slackness and negligence, whatever discontents I was carrying around inside me.

4. *Compassion.* Clearly I was being taught to empathize more deeply with the many Christians, lay and ordained, male and female, who live with various kinds of disappointments, and thus were in the same boat as myself.

5. *Humility.* I must never forget that God is supreme and important and I am neither, and He can manage very well without me whenever He chooses to do so.

God did not leave me in the desert. In due course, with clear guidance, my wife and I emigrated, and today I follow the gleam of the vision He still (as I think) gives me—a vision of reformation and revival—in a larger world than England.

Tabasco sauce (often imitated, never duplicated as the label says) gains its flavor from the oak barrels in which it matures. I suspect that my last years in England were a sort of oak barrel period, but that is for others to judge.

The mother of a school friend was clairvoyant, though as a Christian she wished she were not, and she was unable to tell her genuine second sight from her own wishful thinking. Before I was a believer she assured me that I would end up in Christian ministry, and I remember her also admonishing me in those far-off days that I should need to remember the proverbial wisdom versified by Kipling, "He travels the fastest who travels alone." Her first word was certainly verified; was the second? I cannot tell, though maybe when the books are opened I shall discover. At present, however, it is one of the many things I do not know.

But as a sometime denizen of the desert I have totally verified the wisdom of David's words in Psalm

27:14, "Wait for the LORD; / be strong and take heart and wait for the LORD" (NIV), and that, as I can and do testify, is encouragement enough to be going on with.

chapter 7

I Crashed Hard

Charles Stanley

🌿 DURING SEVERAL YEARS OF STRIVING FOR PERFECTION and seeking approval in my ministry, I knew what I was doing—at least to an extent. I knew at some level of understanding that I was working too hard for an impossible ideal and expecting too much of myself and others. How did I justify my behavior?

Well, I handled it like a perfectionist who was continually seeking approval! I blamed my behavior on everybody else and refused to be critical of myself. I rationalized my behavior by saying, "God made me this way."

The result was that I got on a downward spiral of more and more work in an effort to get better and better and to receive more and more approval. Eventually, I crashed hard. I entered a desert experience with profound consequences for me.

In 1977, I was doing two thirty-minute television programs plus the Sunday morning television program that came from the church, in addition to everything else I was doing as a pastor. I noticed that instead of just being tired on Monday—which is normal for a pastor after having preached Sunday morning and Sunday night—I was tired on Tuesday. Pretty soon I was tired on Wednesday too. Then I realized that I was as tired on Saturday as I was on Monday morning.

I went to the hospital three times that year and had all kinds of tests, and each time, the doctors found nothing wrong. I'd tell my physician, "There's nothing wrong. I'm just tired." I'd try to take a little break, but it was never a long enough break to really help me.

Stephen Olford came to my church one weekend to preach, and on Saturday night my wife and I went with him and his wife to have dinner at a downtown hotel.

We went to the same hotel where we had gone three years before. On that occasion Dr. Olford had told us about the physical problems he had experienced. I remember thinking as he shared his story, *I'm never going to let that happen to me.*

Yet, there we were three years later, and he was asking me, "How are you doing?"

I said, "Fine." My wife said, "No, you're not. Tell him the truth."

So I told him about my exhaustion, and he said, "You're going to the hospital tonight."

I said, "No, I'm not. You're preaching for our Missions Sunday service in the morning, and I've got to be there."

He said, "No, you don't. And furthermore, I'm going to arrange for twelve of the best preachers in the nation to come and preach for you every Sunday for the next three months."

I said, "Oh, I don't know about that."

Dr. Olford did just what he said, however. He, his wife, and my wife, Annie, drove me to the hospital and checked me in. The next morning after he had preached, he called a meeting of the deacons of the church and said to them, "If you want this man alive, you've got to give him a leave of three months, six months—whatever it takes."

He and one of the deacons came to see me in the hospital that same Sunday night, and they said, "We forbid you to come back to preach at the church for at least three months." Dr. Olford then arranged for outstanding preachers to fill the pulpit the next twelve Sundays, a different person each week.

I went from the hospital in Atlanta to a medical center in Virginia for two weeks to have a thorough series of tests. Every morning I had tests, and in the afternoons I'd walk and pray. The doctors didn't find anything physically wrong—no heart problems, no ulcers. I was just worn out.

A caring, generous man in our church arranged for me to go to a small island that was about two and a quarter miles long and a quarter mile at its widest point. The island is located about two hundred miles directly east of West Palm Beach. Only 230 people live on it and there are no hotels, no automobiles, and there were only two telephones at the time. Annie couldn't go with me since we were in the process of building a house. So Andy, my son, took a few weeks leave from his schooling, and he and I went to the island for five weeks. We fished, walked, swam, read, studied, and prayed.

It sounds idyllic.

But when you've been running as fast as you can and you are feeling driven twenty-four hours a day, getting off to an isolated place like that is a shock. Suddenly, there's nothing to drive toward! There's nobody around to applaud you. There's nothing to get up for or to keep you going. It was like hitting a wall.

I also felt so drained that I wondered if I'd ever regain sufficient strength to function normally, and in the midst of this desert I had lots of self-doubt to go along with the exhaustion.

I had no difficulty talking to God, and I certainly didn't place any blame on Him for the situation I was in. I knew that the problem was resident in me. I was feeling driven to succeed. I was committed to so many things, and I didn't know where to get off the wheel that was spinning. I wanted to stop wearing myself out—but I didn't know how to stop doing all that I was doing. I had a sense that I needed to stop overextending myself, but at the same time, I didn't know which activity to drop.

Ultimately, I didn't want to give anything up. I wanted to do everything I was doing. I wanted to achieve everything I was achieving. I'd look at a situation and say to myself, "Well, this is working—so why give that up?" And so it went for everything I was doing.

I don't know why I felt I had to do so much. Perhaps I was trying to prove to myself that I could do everything in which I was involved. Perhaps I was responding to the approval I was receiving. Perhaps it was related to the circumstances facing me in the church at that time.

I had a strong desire to see souls saved and to see the pews of the church filled with people. I had an equally strong desire to make sure that all of the programs at the church functioned to serve the people.

I had big goals in lots of areas and kept them continually in front of me. I had goals for my life, goals for the family, and seven major goals for the church. Short range. Middle range. Long range. I had them all lined up, and I was committed to making them happen, do or die. I had a strong desire to reach those goals as quickly as possible, but I had too little help, and my inner desire to control everything only exacerbated the matter further. When you have that combination of qualities, the tendency is to spread yourself very thin and to become overextended. I had done just that.

The number one person who had put me in this desert wilderness was I!

Now, if you had asked me at the time whether I was driven, I would have said to you, "No, I just love God." In looking back, I realized that much of what I thought I was doing for God, I was really doing for Charles Stanley. Much of my prayer life was focused on what *I* wanted to achieve—what *I* wanted to accomplish for the church.

As a result, often my relationship with God was based primarily on His helping me to get things done. I knew He had the power to do it, and I thought that if I just believed hard enough and trusted Him to act, the goals would be reached.

I don't think I've ever felt I could do anything significant on my own. I frequently told God how inadequate I felt and how I couldn't do anything if He didn't do it. Looking back now, I realize that I was deceived about my motivations. In many ways, the motivations were masked by the success. Things were working! The church was growing! Goals were being met. I didn't want to stop. In point of fact, all seven of the goals I had set for the church to reach by 1990 were reached long before that.

I never asked God for permission to stop any of the activities in which I was involved. I asked Him only for strength to do more.

There's a big difference between enjoying the accomplishment of a goal and enjoying the process of working toward that goal. I enjoyed the results of what I was doing, but I didn't enjoy the activities themselves. For example, I liked the fact that we had a successful thirty-minute television program that came from the pastor's study. But I hated the emotional drain of those programs—doing them three or more at a time, having to concentrate completely on the camera with no audience present, needing to supply all of the emotional energy and strength to carry that type of format.

And in the process of wanting to do it all and have it all, I found myself utterly exhausted physically, mentally, and emotionally.

My island getaway helped me to recover a certain degree of physical and mental strength, so at least a part of my healing had begun by the time I returned to Atlanta. Upon my return, I said to the carpenter who was building our house, "Put me to work." I went over to the construction site every day and worked as a carpenter's helper. Working with my hands for a month was excellent therapy.

Finally, after twelve weeks, I returned to the church. I found attendance up, the offering up, and the people happy. God had taken good care of the flock while I was nowhere to be found—out in the desert.

It took nearly ten more months, however, for me to feel that I was fully back physically. I remember the moment when I stepped into the pulpit and said, "I feel good!"

But there was one other aspect of my desert experience that seemed to snare me like a fly caught in a spider's web.

Over this period of approximately twelve months I benefited from the changes I had made in scheduling—my priorities, my approach to work, and my newfound ability to trust others—but there was a deeper issue.

Although I was rested in my body, and although I had made changes to curb my striving for perfection and approval, I still felt the *need* for perfection and approval. A deep, inner ache still filled my spirit.

Over the years—actually, over the decades—I have confessed and repented thousands of times of everything imaginable. You may ask, "Did you confess the hostility, anger, and bitterness you felt about your childhood?" Yes, I confessed all that, too, and I asked God to forgive me. I fasted, prayed, begged God, pleaded with God, cried out to God, went to seminars—you name it, I have done it. Yet still, nothing satisfied the ache inside me.

If you think that praying, studying the Bible, fasting,

and even working hard at sermons will make you a saint, I'm here to tell you that it doesn't work that way. Trying hard to be healed of inner emotional pain won't free you from it.

Through the years, I occasionally said to Annie, "I sure would hate to die. It's not that I'm afraid to die, I'm just not ready."

One day I added, "There has to be more than I know. I have missed something. There's something I don't know that I've missed, and I've got to find out what it is." At other times I said to her, "There's something between God and me, and I just can't identify what it is. But I know there's something between us."

The ache was especially evident after I preached a series from the Bible entitled, The Truth Can Set You Free. During each week of the series, people throughout the church would come up to me and say, "Pastor, these messages have really set me free."

I'd get home, however, look heavenward on Sunday afternoon and say, "But God, what about me? I'm the one preaching the sermon, and I don't have this freedom in my heart. I know it's Your truth, but I don't know it as a full reality in my life."

The inner pain finally grew unbearable. While I was out preaching in Oregon at a conservative Baptist meeting, everything seemed to come to a head. I would preach for about forty minutes and then quit, but the people would say, "We don't have anyplace to go. Keep on talking." So the meetings were long, and God was blessing those who were there. From the outside looking in, everything seemed very successful. Yet, I went home from that conference discouraged and disheartened and with nobody to blame. In fact, there wasn't a single day in my life about which I could blame anybody or find fault!

Nevertheless, I was miserable to the point of being desperate. God in His mercy led me to call four friends—all of whom are very wise men, and all of whom are younger than I. They are men of highest integrity. I believed they would hear me out with empathy and trust God to help them to help me.

I asked the four men if they would meet me somewhere and just let me talk to them because I was at the end of myself. I didn't know what to do, I didn't know where to go, and I didn't know to whom I could talk.

The four men willingly agreed to meet with me, and

when we gathered together, I asked them if they would let me share with them my life. I told them that anything they advised me to do, I would do. I had that much respect for them. I conveyed to them how desperate I was. They knew I was extremely serious about receiving their counsel.

I talked with them all afternoon and all evening. I woke up several times in the middle of the night and wrote seventeen pages in longhand—legal-sized pages—of things I wanted to be sure to tell them the next morning. I told them everything I remembered about my early life and all the highlights—both painful and positive—of my adult life and ministry. I started with my first memory in life and brought it up to the very moment. When I was finished, I said, "Now, whatever you tell me to do, I'll do it."

They asked me two or three questions, and then one of the men who was sitting directly across the table from me said, "Charles, put your head on the table and close your eyes." I did. He said to me very kindly, "Charles, I want you to envision your father picking you up in his arms and holding you. What do you feel?"

I burst out crying. And I cried and I cried and I cried

and I cried. I could not stop crying. Finally, when I stopped, he asked me again, "What do you feel?" I said, "I feel warm, loved and secure. I feel good." And I started weeping again.

For the first time in my life, I felt emotionally that God loved me. That may come as a shock to you. It shocked me too. I had known God loved me as a fact of His Word. I had believed God loved me, accepting that as the nature of God. But I had never emotionally felt God loving me.

For decades I had preached about trusting God, believing God, obeying God. But when I came home and looked through my sermon file, I discovered that I had preached only one sermon on the love of God (and it wasn't worth listening to). I hadn't preached on God's love because I didn't know what it meant to feel the love of God!

God used that encounter with those four men, and that one simple question, to begin to release me from years of excess baggage that I had been hauling around in my life. The full release didn't happen in a day. It was a process, little by little. But God began to reveal my true identity in Christ—that I belonged to Him as I had

never belonged to anybody, that I was worth something to Him (and the Cross proved that), and that He
loved me beyond measure.

The chasm that had separated me from God wasn't
sin. It was a chasm of damaged emotions—emotions so
hurt and raw that I had been unable to experience the
love of God flowing in my direction.

I discovered at the end of myself a kind and gracious
God who had been loving me unconditionally all my
life. There's nothing as liberating as that discovery! And
that discovery was the final key to my being led out of
the desert into a place of living water and the light and
life of God becoming precious to me.

Desert times can be tough—emotionally and physically, they can be occasions of harshness and loneliness.
Further, from a spiritual perspective they can often
leave you in a wasteland where you feel barren and
dry—longing for living water but finding no source to
quench your thirst. Although we know our kind Father
has not forsaken us, we sometimes feel that He is absent
and we are abandoned.

There are a few pointers I would like to suggest to
you—lessons I have learned from my desert experience:

1. Put yourself in a position of rest. Get away. Take a long enough break for your body to mend, your mind to clear, and your heart to heal.

2. Ask the Lord to show you how to trust Him more. Ask Him to reveal to you specific ways in which you can turn over the authority and responsibility of your life to Him. Ask Him to give you specific ways in which you can lighten the load of your schedule and obligations.

3. If yours is a stress-related burnout problem, admit to the Lord that you are responsible for your burnout tendencies. Ask the Lord to show you what to do about the inner pain and emotional baggage that may be driving you to strive relentlessly for approval and perfection. Ask the Lord to do whatever is necessary in your life for you to get to the place and time where He can heal you and fill your life with His approval, His love, and His presence.

chapter 8

Out of My Wilderness, into God's Love
John Trent, Ph.D.

❧ THE WILDERNESS FOR ME WAS GROWING UP IN a single-parent home and longing for the day when the phone would ring and it would be my father. He had left my mother and brothers when I was only two months old. All my life I had longed to meet him. I longed to talk to him. Longed for him to come to a game. And then the day came during my junior year in high school when the phone finally rang.

"Zoa, this is Joe." The phone call came out of the blue, without warning, without explanation, without an apology for all the years my father hadn't called, hadn't come by, hadn't communicated. "I live over by the stadium where the boys are playing, and I'd sure like to come and meet them. Would that be all right?"

A few days earlier the local newspaper had run an

article about our upcoming game, and a reporter had come to our practice, bringing a photographer with him who took a picture that ended up on the front page of the sports section with this caption: *Jeff and John Trent—Twin Starters for the Mighty Titans.*

The picture is what prompted the phone call. He said he wanted to watch my brother and me play, and then we would all meet on the field afterward. He had played a year of college football before he went to the war, we learned. Now he was coming to watch us play.

The night before the game, I hardly slept. Kickoff finally came, and after a game that seesawed back and forth for three quarters, our team finally went down in defeat.

Neither Jeff nor I was discouraged about the loss. We had played our hearts out, but not for us, not for our team, our coach, or our school. We had played our hearts out for our dad. We wanted him to see the sons he hadn't seen for all of these years, and when he saw them, to be proud.

After the game my mother and older brother came down from the stands to meet us. Together we walked to the place near the end zone where Dad had said he would be. It was a moment we had waited for all of our lives. We took off our helmets, hoping he would see us and somehow recognize us. While the fans streamed from the stands and onto the field, we searched for the hero who had finally fought his way home.

In the final scene of the movie *Field of Dreams*, Ray Kinsella finally sees his father after years of separation. "Look at him," Ray says to his wife. "He's got his whole life in front of him, and I'm not even a glint in his eye. *What do I say to him?*"

What do you say at a moment like that? To a father you have never seen, never met, never talked to? Do you run to him, walk to him, wait for him to walk to you? Do you hug him or shake his hand? What?

As I wondered these things, the crowd thinned, the bus left, the parking lot emptied. Then finally someone shut off the stadium lights, leaving the four of us standing on the field. On that dark, empty field.

He didn't show.

He was my father and a hero . . . and he didn't show.

And that football field turned into a wilderness.

Losing My Way in the Dark

The night the lights went out on the football field, the lights went out on my dreams. I had always thought that the way out of my heartache and hurt—the way out of my wilderness—would happen when I finally met my father. But when he didn't show up, I pretended not to care. Only all the anger I swallowed was like shaking up a bottle of soda pop. I became an explosion waiting to happen.

My callousness turned to harshness. At school one day I beat up a kid just for looking at me. After school I was worse, particularly with my drinking buddies. One night seven of us beat the moody blues out of a carload of longhairs from another school, smashed their car windows, and sped off laughing. I was so drunk I didn't remember much about it. The longhairs, however, did. When the police investigated the incident, they pulled me out of class for questioning. I didn't confess to what I had done, didn't rat on my friends, and shrugged off the lecture they gave me. Most of all, I didn't feel anything for the guys I had whipped. But for the first time I felt something. It wasn't guilt, wasn't shame, wasn't remorse. It was embarrassment.

My life was out of control.

I knew it.

My mom knew it.

Now the whole school knew it.

Like many people without a clear path to follow, I headed deeper into the wilderness . . . and the "curse" it carried.

When You Can't Find Life-Giving Water

In Hebrew, the word *wilderness* is closely linked with the word *curse.* When you hear the word *curse,* don't think of a Stephen King novel or some scary person shaking a bloody chicken leg at you. In the Old Testament, the literal word *curse* was actually a picture of withholding life-giving water from a person. The word literally means a "trickle" or a "dry stream." What does a dried-up stream have to do with being "cursed"?

Imagine that you're a desert dweller. You set off across the hot, barren sands with the knowledge that at the very end of your strength and endurance, you'll come to a spring. It may be rough going, but there's that oasis of life-giving water and priceless shade at the end of your journey. Great hope sustains a heart that knows there's a place of comfort from the barrenness of the wilderness.

But what if you travel through the heat and rocks and thorns of the wilderness and finally arrive at that life-giving spring—and you find it empty. Instead of life-giving water, there's only dust or at best, a muddy, undrinkable trickle. That's a picture of being cursed, of having something that should give you life evaporate before your eyes.

That's what I felt like when the lights went out on the football field and my father never showed up. All my life I'd thought that if I could just meet him, even once, it would be like reaching an oasis. Then his call came, and at long last, I knew my journey in the wilderness was over. Yet at the end of the game, instead of finding those life-enriching words, or even his hug, we ended up in an empty, dried-up stream. Subtraction, not addition. Indifference, not acceptance.

What happens to people like me when they wander in the wilderness and begin to feel like there's no oasis? There are three common traits that wilderness wanderers share. To some degree, I experienced them all.

Three Marks of a Wilderness Wanderer

1. Wilderness Wanderers Learn to Be Hopeless

The first common effect of being in the wilderness was illustrated in a research study done more than twenty years ago at the University of Pennsylvania. For several months two independent studies were done using laboratory dogs. (Thankfully, researchers don't do these kinds of studies anymore!) One group of dogs was put in a "maze" with various hurdles to jump through in order to get to a newly opened can of food. The average hungry dog could quickly navigate the barriers they'd set up, and in less than three minutes, they'd be enjoying dinner.

At the same time, another group of dogs was put in immovable, inescapable, full-body harnesses and given strong electrical shocks. The rationale they gave for this study was to see how blood serum levels changed under stress.

When the "pain" study was concluded, the researchers decided to use these same dogs to run the "maze" test the first group had completed. Like the dogs before them, the experimenters predicted that they'd quickly

jump the barriers like the other dogs and get to the food
. . . but they were wrong.

When the dogs who had been in a *painful, unpre-dictable, inescapable situation* started through the maze
and ran into the first barrier, they didn't climb over the
obstacle as the other dogs had done . . . *they lay down.*

Physically, these dogs had the strength and ability to
get over the obstacles. But what had been shocked out
of them was the confidence or the willingness to even
try to get over the first barrier.

What were the conclusions they drew from this and
a number of other related studies? Namely, if you put
animals in an uncontrollable, unpredictable, painful sit-uation for a long period of time, they can become hope-less—passive, pessimistic, withdrawn, and unwilling to
face and struggle through obstacles to get to a goal.

Tragically, that's not just something that's true of
man's best friend. It's all too common for men and
women who have been under severe stress to walk up
to a barrier that stands between them and freeze up
inside, giving up instead of working through the issue
or problem.

That's the first mark of living in the wilderness.

Instead of actively trying to solve problems, pain can cause a person to become passive, dependent, and depressed. Unfortunately, we can live out two other negative responses as well.

2. Wilderness Wanderers Often Feel
That the Only Way of Escape Lies in the Past

If we've spent too long in the wilderness, in addition to feeling a deep sense of hopelessness, we can also feel that the "one thing" that could change lies in the past.

Take Brian for example. He was the *older* brother and yet his father had lavished all his time and attention on his younger brother. Brian wore his heart out trying to please his father. But no matter what he did, or how much he accomplished, he never could gain the acceptance he wanted so much. Can you see the picture of the dry stream in Brian's life? Wanting so much to have his father's love and affirmation, walking so far in the wilderness, and finding only sand instead of life-giving water every time? Brian felt the only thing that could make his life fulfilling was if he could have been the "younger" brother. But there was no way he could go back in time and become the younger brother. And if the key to a fulfilling life today is dependent on something that we can't go back and change in the past, then we'll stay stuck with our problem and stranded in the wilderness.

I know that because I spent years thinking, *If only . . . If only . . . If only . . .* If only I had been older when my father left . . . maybe I could have talked him into staying. If only he hadn't gone to war and been through so many terrible experiences . . . but the truth is, he had. If only I could have been good enough, or fast enough or smart enough—then maybe the clock would turn back and he would have been a part of our lives. But I couldn't change the past, no matter how long or hard I thought about it. And as long as I put all my focus on what "should have" or "might have" happened, I wasn't "forgetting what lies behind and reaching forward to what lies ahead" (Phil. 3:13 NASB). I wasn't moving out of the wilderness, I was walking deeper into the darkness.

Wilderness wanderers often feel hopeless, and frequently get stuck in the past, wishing and hoping for the impossible instead of taking action today. And there's a third characteristic.

3. Wilderness Wanderers Often
Become Experts at Blaming and Complaining

In the Old Testament, the people in the wilderness were characterized by all their griping and complaining. That's not just an ancient-day activity. A very modern response to growing up deprived of love and acceptance is to deal with the pain by blaming others. The blame game is almost a national pastime, and along with it comes an unwillingness to take responsibility for changes we need to make.

For example, several years ago I was handed a letter that shows the lengths someone can go to keep from taking responsibility for what's wrong in their lives:

I'm 34 years old and I've been married three times. (Not my fault; I always seem to pick losers.) My problem is my hair . . . or lack of it. I know that many men feel there's nothing wrong with being bald, but I do. I started losing my hair when I was in high school and I have tried everything I know since to stop what's happening to me or to reverse it. I know that my first wife left me because of my hair. My latest wife even told me straight out that I was obsessed with my hair and that was why she was leaving. *My lack of hair is ruining my life!* I went to a plastic surgeon recently and offered to pay him in advance to transplant whatever skin I needed to fix my head. All he did was to insult me by saying that I shouldn't waste my money on scalp surgery . . . and spend the money on my head with a psychiatrist! I'm sure that doctor wasn't a Christian. That's why I'm writing you to ask your advice . . .

Grumble and blame. That's a mark of being a wilderness wanderer. Just like feeling "hopeless" or staying focused on the past, instead of a hopeful future.

Is there any hope to get out of the wilderness?

Not if we're relying on the secular self-help shelf or on daytime talk shows to show us the way. Our society won't help us. Even left on our own we'll just keep wandering in circles around the wilderness, the same way the Israelites kept taking laps around the desert. But just like almighty God provided a way out of the wilderness for His people, there is a path today for wilderness wanderers. It's the only true path to freedom from past hurts, and to seeing the "curse" reversed and what was taken away put back in.

In God's words, "The LORD your God would not listen to Balaam, but the LORD your God turned the curse into a blessing for you, because the LORD your God loves you" (Deut. 23:5 NKJV).

I'm convinced it takes the power of almighty God to add the "life-giving water" that significant people in our lives may have withheld or taken from us. Reversing the curse and providing a way out of the wilderness take God's love, forgiveness, power, and patience.

Take it from someone who's been there. It takes more than positive thinking, pulling yourself up by your bootstraps, or the latest psychological fad to "reverse the curse" of a difficult past. It takes God's strength and following God's path to fullness of life and real freedom from sin and death. And for me, I'll be forever thankful for the person who showed me that path.

Out of the Wilderness and into God's Love

No matter how hard I tried to find a way out of the wilderness I was in, I sank deeper into darkness and sin.

That is, until Doug Barram showed me the way of escape. Doug was the local Young Life leader. It was his job to show up at practices, go to games, and lead clubs full of singing and skits and messages about accepting Christ.

I wasn't interested in the sermons. But what I couldn't explain away was the smile on this big, six-foot-three-inch ex–offensive lineman who befriended so many of my friends. He would invite a bunch of us to "club," and even over to his home for big spaghetti dinners. Reluctantly at first, I'd go for the food. But I always went away with more in my heart than in my stomach.

The first time I ever prayed with a group of people was around Doug's table. You had to join hands and pray for the food before you ate at the Barrams'. I had prayed things like, "God, if You get me out of this one . . . ." But I'd never prayed the way he did. It was so *real* to him.

I'd watch him love on his wife and children—really love them. I saw for the first time the incredible peace and security and love that come from a man sold out to the Person he talked about each week in club—Jesus.

And then Doug took my brother Jeff and me to a

Billy Graham movie. I didn't know what that meant at the time, and I certainly would have never gone if I'd known it was a "religious" film. It was called *For Pete's Sake,* and while I didn't like the movie, I couldn't help but see in the main character's life the same kind of faith I'd seen all that year in Doug's life.

And then, suddenly, I could see two paths.

Even as the movie ended and a man stood up and invited people to come to Christ, I could see that I stood at a crossroads. If I kept going the way I was headed, I'd go deeper into the wilderness. Farther into darkness and anger and sin. And then I looked down our row and saw Doug. And suddenly I knew that coming to Jesus meant following the same road Doug had chosen as a young man. A road that led to the Cross and to a Savior who wanted to cleanse me of all that anger, all that hurt, and all the hurt I had caused others.

I never knew Jesus came in a six-foot-three-inch frame, but I saw Jesus in Doug that night. And I knew that if I wanted Jesus inside my life, I'd have to make the same decision he had.

Slowly, I stood up to go forward, and as I looked beside me, my brother Jeff had stood up too. So had two of our friends and fellow football players whom Doug had brought to the movie. And so four angry, rebellious, partying, lonely, hurting young men walked down a theater aisle that night and asked Jesus to forgive them and come into their hearts. That night four young men walked into a theater, out of their wilderness, and into God's light.

As a footnote, all four of those young men—now middle-aged men with teenagers of their own—still love Jesus and still love Doug Barram. As for Doug? He still works with inner-city kids in the prison system today in Washington State—still loving unlovable kids like we were one at a time—and telling them that in Jesus there is a way out of their wilderness.

To read the whole story of how I walked out of the wilderness and, through God's power, "reversed the curse" for me, see *Pictures the Heart Remembers*, John Trent, Ph.D., WaterBrook Press, 2000.

chapter *9*

A Winter's Tale

Sheila Walsh

See, I am doing a new thing!

Now it springs up; do you not perceive it?

I am making a way in the desert

    and streams in the wasteland. (Isa. 43:19 NIV)

The cold wind howls across the wasteland of my soul.

Barren. Bitter. Strong.

All memory of flowers gone.

The cold wind howls across the wasteland of my soul.

There is silence in the ruins,

Save the Winter's mourning song.

❦ AS A CHILD GROWING UP ON THE WEST COAST OF
Scotland, I was fascinated by the concept of the desert,
for I lived in a hilly land. To the east was the cold, gray
ocean. To the west, north, and south were hills and more

hills covered with yellow gorse bushes and purple and white heather. Only rugged flowers and bushes could survive the wind. I loved the rich, earthy tapestry of Scottish soil, well-watered by frequent rain. As I think of my childhood now I think of green lush grass, gray skies, and standing at the bus stop in the rain with wet feet, playing hopscotch in the puddles. Even the summer months were graced with frequent showers or what my grandmother referred to as "drizzle." This was a light mist of rain that seemed harmless enough but could soak you to the skin in moments. I look back at old family photographs and smile. There we were on the beach in the summer months, free of school at last, wrapped up to the neck in warm sweaters. I remember watching *Lawrence of Arabia* on our black-and-white television one wet Saturday afternoon and marveling at the endless expanse of sand and sunshine. It seemed perfect to me as a melancholic child. I would lie in my bed at night, the west coast wind rattling the windowpanes and howling round the eaves of the house, and dream of space and sand and sun.

So when I was twenty-four years old I took my meager savings as a Youth for Christ worker into a travel agency and asked if I had enough to go to Africa. It was time to visit the desert. I set off by myself for Tunisia, Northern Africa, leaving behind a mother on her knees who was convinced I would be abducted into white slavery. I would not be deterred.

As the plane began its descent into Tunis airport, I saw the land of my dreams rise to meet me. I spent the first few days exploring my surroundings and drinking in the mellow golden rays of winter sun. Then I was ready. The hotel where I was staying had arranged for two Bedouins to take me by camel across part of the Northern Sahara Desert. The Bedouins, I was told, were Arabian tent dwellers. They seemed the perfect guides. My camel, however, was a malcontent in need of a good bath and a lesson in etiquette. He spat, grunted, and was able to blow his tongue up like an off-color party balloon. One of my guides carried on a constant dialogue with him. "You be a good camel. Lady give me big tip." The camel seemed above the lure of avarice.

The moment I had been waiting for left me breathless and speechless. It even silenced the camel. It was the sunrise over the Sahara. The morning sun appeared as an enormous ball of fire that seemed to rise from the earth and ignite every grain of sand. It was a holy moment. The God who had made all this was my Father, and even though I was far away from home, in a spectacular wasteland, I was in the palm of His hand. I would remember the impact of that moment ten years later. I would need that reassurance; for not all deserts are touched by sun.

> I am like a desert owl,
>> like an owl among the ruins. (Ps. 102:6 NIV)

My friend Thelma Wells plants artificial flowers in her yard. She wants the color and gaiety of rampant blossoms but has neither the time nor the temperament to cultivate that in the land of the living. She waters them. They move in the breeze. The only giveaway from a distance would be if you watched a bee land on one of the flowers. As soon as it lands, it is gone. There is no life there. The flowers have nothing to give. I wonder now if that is how I seemed to those who stopped by my life in 1992 for nurture and sustenance?

On the surface I was one of the best producers in God's yard. I was the cohost of *The 700 Club* on the Christian Broadcasting Network (CBN). I traveled on weekends to speak and sing. I wrote books. The staff at

CBN knew that they could come into my office and tell me anything and I would pray for them. Their story would never leave the four walls of my office. But I was like one who lived within walls of her own making. I was able to reach over and comfort others but there was no way back to me. No one was allowed to look too closely. At some core level I believed that my worth to God and man was that I was a strong, caring woman who had her act together. I wanted desperately to be accepted, but I sensed that the real me was unacceptable.

Now as I tuck my three-year-old son, Christian, into bed, I wonder when it was that I decided I would not do it all. When did I determine that life was not safe, that no one loves you forever, that "ministry" is the best place in the world to hide? I watch him as he sleeps. His little mouth moves like a baby fish. A smile across his face. Every day I tell him he is the most beautiful boy in the world, and he believes it. He loves his life and is thoroughly entertained by himself. On a recent flight I watched as he attempted to pull a reluctant traveler into his world. He pulled out his best impersonations, animal noises, and funny faces. When the man retreated behind the *Wall Street Journal,* Christian looked at me as if to say,

"What is wrong with *him*?" He knew he had performed up to snuff, so what was that man's problem? Somewhere along the road I lost that sense of being okay. We all do. It's part of growing up, but I exchanged it for a weighty overcoat of shame.

Was it when my father's brain hemorrhage altered his personality and he became a confusing presence in our house?

Was it the messages we all hear as we grow up that we don't quite "fit in," that we're not quite "acceptable"?

Was it the subtle realization that as long as you are in "ministry," others will assume that everything in your garden is well? And was it realizing that's how they wanted it to be; indeed, why you were valued at all?

All I know is that I was slowly dying inside. I was lonely. I was afraid. I was unbearably sad. What added to my hopelessness was the fact that I had no idea what was wrong with me. I loved God. I enjoyed serving Him. I believed He loved me. Some nights I would drive out of the gates of CBN and turn my car toward the ocean. I would park at the far end of the beach and get out and walk and walk for miles. I can remember sitting on a sand dune, gripping my knees to my chest and groaning from a place too deep inside for me to understand. I decided that I was losing my mind. My father had died in his thirties in a bleak psychiatric hospital in Scotland. That legacy seemed to be imprinted on my soul, "Like father, like daughter."

I remember sitting in Pat Robertson's office asking for a leave of absence, telling him that I had been accepted as a patient in a psychiatric unit in a hospital in Washington, D.C. I was filled with the shame that is peculiar to those who struggle with mental illness. He was kind to me, gentle and understanding. He wanted one of the staff to drive the four-hour trip to the hospital and check me in. I said no. I couldn't bear the thought of anyone seeing me walk through those doors that would lock behind me. I went alone. After the indignities of check-in, where you are stripped of anything that could potentially hurt you or anyone else, I was shown to my room. I sat on the floor all night. *I am like a desert owl, like an owl among the ruins.*

I have never felt more alone or more desolate in my life. It was cold and wet outside. Once more the wind shook the windowpanes of my room, only this time they were locked. I still had my Bible. I opened it to the Psalms, looking for drops of water in the wasteland. I turned to the end of Psalm 27. "I am still confident of this: / I will see the goodness of the LORD / in the land of the living" (Ps. 27:13 NIV).

I read those words as if God had added them as I drove to the hospital. I was raised in the church. My undergraduate degree is in theology, but I had no memory of ever reading those words before. They seemed to me as a mirage. They were what I wanted to see, what I needed to survive, but I knew if I reached out for them they would dissipate like an oasis in the desert.

My greatest fear as I was growing up was that I would end up in a place like my father. What I did not know then was that God had planned to deliver me from myself in the ruins of my life. I did not understand then that some of God's most precious gifts come in boxes that make your hands bleed when you open them. Inside is what you have been longing for all your life. Only God could do that. Only God would do that. Only His love is as fierce and relentless as our deepest pain, our unspoken fears. We become accustomed to simply surviving. God wants more.

Perhaps even as you read these words you are tempted to put this book down as the wind begins to rattle the bars of your life. I understand that. Change is terrifying.

There are doors in our lives we have locked so tight, we are convinced that if we were to open them we would be consumed by what is inside. We would be left alone. But that's the whole, glorious point: *We are not alone.* I discovered that on that rainy night in October of 1992 when I checked into the hospital. I thought I checked in alone. I wanted to check in alone. But Christ checked in with me. He sat with me, all night, on the floor.

I will never forget that first morning. I stood in the patients' lounge, looking at my feet, unsure what to do. I don't know what I expected, but this was definitely not it. I remember as a young girl watching a movie called *The Snake Pit.* I had nightmares for weeks. It portrayed a psychiatric institution at its most primal, most barbaric state. As I looked around me now, no one was rending their clothes in two, beating their heads against the walls, or having conversations with Elvis.

As the days turned into a week, then two weeks, what I discovered was a group of people very like myself. They were people who loved God but didn't have all the answers. They were people who were struggling to come to terms with their humanity lived out in imperfect bodies: A pastor who had nothing left to say to his people. A teacher who had lost hope in the future, whose futility had rendered her impotent to give anything at all to her students. A young girl whose only perceived area of control was to starve herself; the success of her rebellion was killing her. And me. My office back in Virginia was knee-deep in letters from viewers who told me how God had used me to help them understand how passionately He loved them. That seemed ironic. As deep as the marrow of my bones I felt unloved and unlovable. For the first few days my counselors tried to help me wade through a sea of emotions. What I discovered under the anger and sadness was a paralyzing fear.

> There is no fear in love. But perfect love drives out fear, because fear has to do with punishment. The one who fears is not made perfect in love. (1 John 4:18 NIV)

I read those words as I sat in the small garden of the hospital grounds. I remembered hearing them from Academy Award–winning songwriter Al Kasha just a few weeks before. I was interviewing him, discussing his battle with agoraphobia. He said, "I discovered that just as perfect love casts out fear, we can allow our fear to cast out God's perfect love."

Was that me? Was I so afraid of my "not good enoughness" that I kept God's perfect love standing at the front door? It would have been easier if I had some terrible sin to confess, what we consider with our skewed human sight to be one of the "big ones." But all I had was me and a sense that I was not enough. I was right. That was the bad news and good news rolled into one spectacular gift. I *wasn't* enough. Even in all my supposed best moments I wasn't enough and I never would be. Christ is enough. He loved me completely, shadows and all. That hit me one morning as I sat with several of the patients and nurses in a small church. It wasn't a remarkable service or a particularly new sermon topic, but I was raw and open; my defenses were down. And deep in my soul I heard and I believed, "You are loved. You are loved. You are loved." I wept the exhausted tears of one who has been wandering alone in the desert for years and finally catches sight of the way home. There was no quick fix or dramatic rescue, just the relief of finding Christ, the Way.

I'll never forget the words of one of my counselors:

"Sheila, Christ did not come to get you out of this but to live in you through it." And so they gave me a spiritual compass, pointed north, and said, "This is the way home." I left the hospital vulnerable, weak but alive.

> A voice of one calling:
> "In the desert prepare
>   the way for the LORD;
> make straight in the wilderness
>   a highway for our God." (Isa. 40:3 NIV)

In the desert, prepare the way for the Lord. This was a new thought for me. I always read those words as, "A voice of one calling in the desert: 'Prepare the way for the LORD.'" Now I read these words differently: "In the middle of your desert experience, prepare the way for the Lord."

I didn't know where to begin. I had based most of my Christian life on all the things I could do for God. Now I had nothing. I was empty-handed. I was like a newborn child learning how to live. I was living a divine paradox. I had never felt less worthy and yet more loved. I had never been so disenfranchised yet more welcomed by the Father. I began to realize that I had spent most of my life trying to make God glad He chose me. I had run myself into the ground because I wanted to be invaluable. Now there was nothing good left to say about myself, and even if there had been I was too tired to say it.

There seems to be something that the desert alone can gift us with. Perhaps it's because there are no other distractions. Perhaps it's the very aloneness, the silence, that makes us finally listen to all the rumblings in our souls. I think now, How kind of God to let all my greatest fears happen rather than simply to remove them. I longed for a rescue; He gave me a relationship. I wanted deliverance; He gave me companionship in the ruins. If He had simply removed my fears I would have lived the rest of my life dreading their return. To let them happen and sit with me, bloodied and bruised, was the most precious gift of love. I cried a lot. I cried for months. Sometimes they were tears of sadness for the loss of all I perceived to be true. Sometimes tears of regret. Often they were tears of the purest joy I had ever known. It is the greatest desire of every human being to be loved, to be accepted. Now I understood that I was. It was a weighty gift. I was a hundred and five years old. I was five years old.

In a desert land he found him,
    in a barren and howling waste.
He shielded him and cared for him;
    he guarded him as the apple of his eye. (Deut. 32:10 NIV)

I began to live differently. I began to tell what was actually true rather than what I wished were true. I went back to seminary like a thirsty child, like a blind man gifted with new eyes. In talking with other survivors of the desert, even though our individual circumstances are different, there are communal gifts. You do not come out of the desert empty-handed. You come out with a pocketful of gifts that are to share. For with love comes grace. I knew the word, but I had no concept of the tidal wave of healing that grace brings to a broken heart.

A girl was sitting on a bus reading Scott Peck's *The Road Less Traveled*. The man beside her asked if it was a good book. She said that it was and continued reading. He asked what it was about. She turned to the contents page and read the list of chapters, "Discipline, Love, Grace."

"What's grace?" he asked.

"I don't know. I haven't gotten to that yet."

That was me. I knew it was in the book, I just hadn't

gotten to it yet. Grace is impossible to grasp outside of the framework of the love of God. It makes no sense. It's as Lewis Smedes described in his book *Shame and Grace:* "The gift of being declared worthy, before we become worthy."[1] What a gift, but how contrary to how we live our lives in this world, in the church, where proving yourself is everything.

At the moment I began to grasp hold of grace, I was as the prodigal son with his well-rehearsed speech drowned out by the love of his father. There is no quid pro quo with God. We have nothing to give, nothing to barter with. He has and is everything. I now believe that God delights to use those of us who have had our hearts and wills broken in the desert, who understand that if we stood in front of the Red Sea and it parted we should get on our faces and worship, not call a press conference.

I remember as an enthusiastic, evangelical teenager reading Paul's words: "I know that nothing good lives in me, that is, in my sinful nature. For I have the desire to do what is good, but I cannot carry it out" (Rom. 7:18 NIV). I foolishly thought, *How modest of Paul. After all, he did write quite a portion of the Bible, so that has to tell you something.* It does, but everything it says speaks to the grace of God to pour eternal things through temporal bodies and perfect truth through bruised hearts and minds. Not a moment of our lives is wasted in God's economy. Even as the blood stops dripping from our wounds, we turn to see that we are being followed by another thirsting for words of life to stanch the flow. The words God spoke to me in the desert were to become my loaves and fishes. They formed the lunch that I could bring to Christ in the presence of the starving masses of His people.

In 1997 I began to travel as one of six speakers with Women of Faith, a national women's conference. From New York to Los Angeles I heard familiar wails. I heard the desolate cry of those who long to be loved and are terrified at the very thought. Twenty thousand women would pack the arenas each weekend, longing to drop that same overcoat of shame and yet wondering, if they did, what would be left of them. And so six women, desert survivors all, stand and let the water of life soak thirsty ground. All we do is sop up. God does the rest. The desert leaves you with the absolute conviction that there is nothing you can do to make God love you and nothing you can do to negate that love. You are left with the liberating awareness that all we are in our best moments are earthen vessels to contain the grace and glory of God. I heard the same song over and over:

- "Thank you for giving me permission to be human."
- "For the first time, I feel as if I am not alone."
- "I have been to church all my life. Tonight I finally understood that Jesus loves me."
- "God knows my whole story and loves me anyway—Hallelujah!"

The amazing thing was that my brokenness was a far greater bridge to others than my apparent wholeness had ever been. If you talk to the desert people you will hear a constant refrain: "I would never have chosen this path but I would not change a single day."

> He turned the desert into pools of water
> and the parched ground into flowing springs.
> (Ps. 107:35 NIV)

Everywhere I turned I was faced with those marked by the blight of the desert sun and changed forever by the journey. I found myself sitting around a table in Littleton, Colorado, with four women whose children's lives had been indecently interrupted by two teenagers with an arsenal of weapons. Even as I listened, almost paralyzed by the thought of this unspeakable terror made so much more real by the presence of these mothers than by any television news report, I heard a familiar refrain.

"Even in my darkest moments, it was as if a snow globe of the grace of God covered me. I will never be the same."

Farther down the path I sat beside a woman about my age. We were at a brunch given in appreciation of those who support the work of the House of Hope, a home for teenage runaways and throwaways in Orlando, Florida.

"Hi. My name is Debbie Arden."

I didn't recognize her name. I didn't know then that her husband was the golf agent for Payne Stewart. I didn't know then that he had also gone down in the plane that took Payne and a few friends to an icy grave. As she told me her story, I looked in her eyes, and there was the unmistakable mark of one who has wrestled with God in the desert and come out with an undying allegiance to Him.

I asked her to imagine this scenario the night before the crash: The doorbell rings. A stranger stands on the doorstep. Somehow you are not afraid, for you sense this is a messenger from God. But the message is an unwelcome one. He tells you that the sand has run out of your husband's glass. Tomorrow will be his last day bound in a human frame. You are not faced with unspeakable news on the telephone or on the TV, but rather a messenger from God Himself brings this decimating news in advance. I asked an unanswerable question: "How do you imagine you would have responded?"

Her answer was fast and fierce: "There is no doubt. I would have crawled under the covers of my bed and never recovered."

But in reality there was no warning. No angel. No time to gather her mind before it was tossed to the four winds of despair. And here is the mystery. I sat in awed silence as Debbie spoke.

"God used the death of my beloved husband to, as Oswald Chambers said, 'Pierce a hole in the darkness so that I could behold the face of God.' I am a changed woman."

God won her heart in the crucible of her worst nightmare.

A Winter's Tale

I began this story with a visual photograph of a pivotal moment in my life: the sunrise over the Sahara.

When I realized that the God who made all this array of splendor around me was my Father and that even though I was far away from home then, in a spectacular wasteland, I was in the palm of His hand. I remembered the impact of that moment ten years later. I needed that reassurance then and now, for not all deserts are touched by sun. But all deserts are inhabited by God.

Some deserts give release on this earth. Some take us all the way home. I saw that in the spring of 1999 as my husband, Barry, and I nursed his mother, Eleanor, through the final stages of liver cancer. This was a bitter desert for her. She did not want to die. She had much to live for. She had a grandchild. A promise for the future. But there was no physical respite this side of heaven. Our prayers and pleadings fell like a fine mist on acres of dry sand. This was not to be the season for rain. Yet even as I sat by her side through the long nights interrupted by pain and morphine and hymns and tears and prayers, there was the unmistakable aroma of the presence of Christ in broken places, so tangible we were silenced by the gift. Her favorite hymn was penned by Martin Luther. We sang it together through the night just days before her death. She sang with strength she did not

have. I sang with tears I could not quench. We held hands
in the desert and raised our voices.

> A mighty fortress is our God,
> A bulwark never failing;
> Our helper He, amid the flood
> Of mortal ills prevailing:
> For still our ancient foe
> Doth seek to work us woe;
> His craft and pow'r are great,
> And, armed with cruel hate,
> On earth is not His equal.
> Did we in our strength confide,
> Our striving would be losing;
> Were not the right Man on our side,
> The Man of God's own choosing:
> Dost ask who that may be?
> Christ Jesus, it is He;
> Lord Sabaoth, His name,
> From age to age the same,
> And He must win the battle.
>
> And tho' this world, with devils filled,
> Should threaten to undo us,

We will not fear, for God hath willed
His truth to triumph thro' us:
The Prince of Darkness grim,
We tremble not for him;
His rage we can endure,
For lo, his doom is sure,
One little word shall fell him.

That word above all earthly pow'rs,
No thanks to them, abideth;
The Spirit and the gifts are ours
Thro' Him who with us sideth:
Let goods and kindred go,
This mortal life also;
The body they may kill:
God's truth abideth still,
His kingdom is forever.

No Fear of Winter

The words of the psalmist David were fresh and new to me in 1992: "I am still confident of this: / I will see the goodness of the LORD / in the land of the living" (Ps. 27:13 NIV).

When you start at the beginning of the psalm it becomes clear why David believed in spring. It is why I believe in spring. It is why I urge you to step out into the desert wasteland with God. You will never be the same.

> The LORD is my light and my salvation—
> > whom shall I fear?
> The LORD is the stronghold of my life—
> > of whom shall I be afraid? (Ps. 27:1 NIV)

> Father of Winter,
> Father of Spring,
> Into your outstretched hands we come.
> Beyond all we know, we come.
> Beyond all we are, we come.
> Meet us in this desert place.
> Change us as we see your face.
> Amen.

Notes

Chapter 3

1. Lewis Smedes, *Shame and Grace* (Harper San Francisco, 1993).
2. Dag Hammarskjold, *Markings* (New York: Knopf, 1964), 58.
3. Henri J. M. Nouwen, *The Wounded Healer* (New York: Doubleday, 1979), 40.

Chapter 9

1. Lewis Smedes, *Shame and Grace* (Harper San Francisco, 1993).